ENJOYING INTIMACY
with
GOD

ENJOYING INTIMACY with GOD

J. OSWALD SANDERS

This Billy Graham Evangelistic Association
special edition is published with permission from
Discovery House Publishers.

Discovery House Publishers

Books, music, and videos that feed the soul with the Word of God

Box 3566 Grand Rapids, MI 49501

Library of Congress Cataloging in Publication Data
Sanders, John Oswald, 1902-1992
    Enjoying intimacy with God.

    Includes bibliographical references.
    1. God—Worship and love. I. Title.
BV4817.S23   248.4   80-21393
ISBN 0-913367-19-2

TO

*the St. Chrischona churches
of Switzerland and Germany*

Contents

Preface

We cannot read the biographies or come within the orbit of great men and women of God, who so obviously enjoy intimacy with Him, without wistfully desiring to share such an experience.

And yet, the soiled, hectic world in which we live is no friend to such aspirations. Time for the cultivation of intimate fellowship seems to be in perennially short supply. Or is it the intensity of desire that is lacking? We can usually manage to find time for what we *really* want to do.

These pages, which touch on only a few aspects of a vast and important area of truth, are sent out in hope that they might bring some encouragement to other fellow seekers after a deeper intimacy with God and His Christ.

What matters supremely, therefore, is not, in the last analysis, the fact that I know God, but the larger fact which underlies it—the fact that **He knows me.** *I am graven on the palms of His hands; I am never out of His mind. All my knowledge of Him depends on His sustained initiative in knowing me. I know Him because He first knew me and continues to know me. He knows me as a friend . . . .*
There is tremendous relief in knowing that His love to me is utterly realistic based at every point on prior knowledge of the worst about me, so that no discovery can now disillusion Him about me.[1]

J. I. Packer

1

Four Circles of Intimacy with God

Exodus 33:7-11

It is an incontrovertible fact that some Christians seem to experience a much closer intimacy with God than others. They appear to enjoy a reverent familiarity with Him that is foreign to us. Is it a matter of favoritism or caprice on the part of God? Or do such people qualify in some way for that desirable intimacy?

Frances Havergal envisioned such a life of deepening intimacy:

> And closer yet, and closer the golden
>   bonds shall be
> Enlinking all who love our Lord in pure
>   sincerity;
> And wider yet, and wider shall the circling
>   glory glow
> As more and more are taught of God, that
>   mighty love to know.

Are there secrets we may discover that would admit us to a similar intimacy? Our aim will be to answer that question.

Both Scripture and experience teach that it is we, not God, who determine the degree of intimacy with Him that we enjoy. We are at this moment *as close to God as we really choose to be*. True, there are times when we would *like* to know a deeper intimacy, but when it comes to the point, we are not prepared to pay the price involved. The qualifying conditions are more stringent and exacting than we are prepared to meet; so we settle for a less demanding level of Christian living.

Everything in our Christian life and service flows from our relationship with God. If we are not in vital fellowship with Him, everything else will be out of focus. But when our communion with Him is close and real, it is gloriously possible to experience a growing intimacy.

In both Old and New Testaments, there are examples of four degrees of intimacy experienced by God's people. In the Old Testament, it is Moses' and the nation of Israel's experience with their God. In the New Testament, it is that of the disciples and their Lord. In each case, the growing intimacy arose out of a deepening revelation of the divine character.

Dr. J. Elder Cumming contended that "in almost every case the beginning of new blessing is a new revelation of the character of God—more beautiful, more wonderful, more precious."[2] This was certainly true in the case of Moses.

MOSES ON THE MOUNTAIN

On several occasions God summoned Moses to ascend Mount Sinai to have fellowship with Him. Twice, the conference lasted for forty days. On one of those occasions, the people of the nation were associated with him. A study of the circumstances reveals that four circles of intimacy developed.

THE OUTER CIRCLE (Exod. 19:11-12)

As the Law was about to be given, God told Moses to prepare the nation for His manifestation on Mount Sinai. They would see His visible presence, but there were limits beyond which they must not pass.

> Let them be ready for the third day, for on the third day the Lord will come down on Mount Sinai in the sight of all the people. And you shall set bounds for the people all around, saying, "Beware that you do not go up on the mountain."

The people could *approach* the mountain, but they could not *ascend* it, on pain of death. Barriers were erected to keep them at a distance from God. "Moses alone, however, shall come near to the LORD, but they shall not come near, nor shall the people come up with him" was the divine dictum (Exod. 24:2).

Why the exclusiveness? The subsequent reactions of the people clearly demonstrated that they were neither qualified for nor desirous of coming too close to God. There were obviously conditions for a fresh revelation of God. They did have a vision of God, but to them "the glory of the LORD was like a consuming fire on the mountain top"(Exod. 24:17).

THE SECOND CIRCLE (Exod. 24:9-11)

> Then Moses went up with Aaron, Nadab and Abihu, and seventy of the elders of Israel, and they saw the God of Israel. . . . They beheld God, and they ate and drank.

That group pressed past the barriers that excluded the rest of the nation and had a much more intimate vision of God than the people: "Under His feet there appeared to be a pavement of sapphire, as clear as the sky itself." They had a limited vision of God in His transcendence, a glimpse of the Eternal. It was probably a theophany. "They beheld God, and they ate and drank."

They must have felt a very real and conscious sense of the divine presence. Their experience was far in advance of that of the people, but *it effected no permanent transformation*. Only a short time later, they were found worshiping the golden calf. They had a vision of God but showed that they were not qualified to ascend to the top of the mountain into deeper fellowship with God.

THE THIRD CIRCLE (Exod. 24:13-14)

> So Moses arose with Joshua his servant, and Moses went up
> to the mountain of God. But to the elders he said, "Wait here
> for us until we return to you."

How quickly the numbers dwindled as the mountain path
grew steeper! Of all Israel, only two qualified for inclusion in
the third circle of intimacy. What was Joshua's special qual-
ification for that privilege? A clue is given in Exodus 33:10-11:
"When all the people saw the pillar of cloud standing at the
entrance of the tent, all the people would arise and worship.
. . . Thus the LORD used to speak to Moses face to face, just as
a man speaks to his friend. When Moses returned to the
camp, his servant Joshua, the son of Nun, a young man,
would not depart from the tent."

The tent was the place where the Shekinah glory rested,
and where God manifested Himself to His people. "Joshua
. . . would not depart from the tent." As Moses' servant, he
would have many errands to go on and services to perform,
but whenever he was free from those duties, he made his
way to the tent. He wanted to be where God manifested
Himself. He would have been present on many occasions
when the Lord spoke to Moses face to face; thus he enjoyed
an intimacy with God excelled only by that of his leader,
Moses. Although he fell short of the vision granted to
Moses, he ascended higher on the glory-covered mountain
than any of his contemporaries. The lesson for us does not
need to be spelled out.

THE INNER CIRCLE (Exod. 24:15-17)

> Then Moses went up to the mountain, and the cloud covered
> the mountain. And the glory of the LORD rested on Mount
> Sinai, and the cloud covered it for six days; and on the
> seventh day He called to Moses from the midst of the cloud.

The divine summons must have filled Moses with awe as he
climbed alone, for "the glory of the LORD was like a consuming fire on the mountain top" (v. 17). The people in the outer

circle saw only the consuming fire and feared. Moses saw in it the glory of God and worshiped.

MOSES EXPERIENCED A DEEPENING INTIMACY OF COMMUNION WITH GOD

"Thus the LORD used to speak to Moses face to face, just as a man speaks to his friend" (Exod. 33:11). "With him will I speak mouth to mouth" (Num. 12:8, KJV*). What could be more intimate—friend to friend, face to face, mouth to mouth! Is there any parallel to that in our experience?

HE SHARED THE DIVINE PERSPECTIVE

He was daring enough to make the request, "Let me know Thy ways" (Exod. 33:13). He desired to know his Friend's principles of action, to share His purposes, and God opened His heart to Moses and revealed something of His own inner nature.

HE EXPERIENCED A SEARCHING TEST IN THE AREA OF AMBITION

When the nation turned to worship the golden calf in Moses' absence, God's anger was kindled, and He said to Moses, "Now leave me alone so that My anger may burn against them and that I may destroy them. *Then I will make you into a great nation*" (Exod. 32:10, NIV†, italics added). Moses' integrity and disinterested love for his people found expression in his audacious response to the divine proposition: "But now, please forgive their sin—but if not,then blot me out of the book You have written" (Exod. 32:32, NIV). The intensity and selflessness of his intercession grew out of his growing intimacy with God. Not only did he refuse to profit at their expense, but he was willing to sacrifice his privileged position in their favor.

HE HAD A SURPASSING REVELATION OF GOD'S GLORY

Communion with God kindled in Moses an intense desire to

---

*King James Version.
†*New International Version.*

know Him better. "I pray Thee, show me Thy glory" was his request (Exod. 33:18). God's answer gave him, and us, an insight into the nature of His glory: I Myself will make all My goodness pass before you, and will proclaim the name of the LORD before you. . . . The LORD, the LORD God, compassionate and gracious, slow to anger, and abounding in loving-kindness and truth; who keeps loving-kindness for thousands, who forgives iniquity, transgression and sin; yet He will by no means leave the guilty unpunished" (Exod. 33:19; 34:6-7).

God's goodness and glory are enshrined in His name, in His moral character. Moses did not see the full glory of God in its unveiled effulgence—only the afterglow that He left behind as He passed by (Exod. 33:20-23).

SOME OF GOD'S GLORY RUBBED OFF ON MOSES

"When Moses was coming down from Mount Sinai . . . Moses did not know that the skin of his face shone *because of his speaking with Him*" (Exod. 34:29, italics added). That is still the divine prescription for radiance.

Had we lived in those Old Testament times, in which group would we be found? With the crowd? The seventy-four? The two? The one?

JESUS AND HIS DISCIPLES

From among those early followers who had evidenced their faith in Him, Jesus chose seventy and sent them out two by two to preach for Him. Later, after a night of prayer, He chose twelve to be with Him for training—to learn His ways and imbibe His spirit. Within the twelve, there emerged a circle of three with whom Jesus became especially intimate. They were closer to Him than any of the others. Within the circle of three, there was one who appropriated the special place on Jesus' breast, and through whom the disciples channeled questions to the Master (John 13:25). "He, leaning back thus on Jesus' breast" is the way John described his privileged position. Seventy, twelve, three, one! In which group would we be found? Each of the disciples was as close to Jesus as he chose to be, for the Son of God had no favorites. We are similarly self-classifying.

G. Campbell Morgan wrote concerning the special three:

> There can be no doubt that these men, Peter, James and John, were the most remarkable in the apostolate. Peter loved Him; John He loved; James was the first to seal his testimony with his blood. Even their blunders proved their strength. They were the men of enterprise; men who wanted thrones and places of power. . . . Mistaken ideas, all of them, and yet proving capacity for holding the keys and occupying the throne. What men from among that first group reign today as these men?

On four special occasions, Jesus admitted them to experiences from which they learned precious lessons. On the occasion of *the raising of Jairus' daughter* (Luke 8:51), they were granted a preview of their Lord's mastery over death and saw His gentleness with the little lass.

On the mount of transfiguration (Matt. 17:1), they gained clearer insight into the importance of His impending death, although they grasped its significance very inadequately (Luke 18:34). There, too, they had a preview of His glory and majesty. "We beheld His glory," recalled John (1:14). "We . . . were eyewitnesses of His majesty," said Peter (1:16).

On the Mount of Olives (Mark 13:3), they marveled at His prophetic discernment, as He shared with them the sweep of the divine purposes and the inner secrets of God.

In the Garden of Gethsemane (Matt. 26:37), they glimpsed in the sufferings of the Savior something of the cost of their salvation, although they were at a loss to interpret His agony.

Those were some of the privileges of the inner circle. Could any of the twelve have been among that favored group? Were the three specially selected by the Lord? With Him there is no caprice or favoritism. Their relationship with Him was the result of their own choice, conscious or unconscious. It is a sobering thought that we too are as close to Christ as we really choose to be.The deepening intimacy of the three with Jesus was the result of the depth of their response to His love and training.

They recognized that intimacy with Him involved responsibility as well as conferred privilege. The Master had told them that "whoever does the will of God, he is My brother and sister and mother" (Mark 3:35). There are some ties that are closer even than those of kinship.

What excluded some disciples from the inner circle? If *perfection* were the criterion, then Peter the denier and James and John the place-seekers would have been excluded. But they were included. If it were *temperament*, then surely the volatile Peter, and James and John the fire-eaters would not have found entrance.

Why then did John have the primacy in the group? Because he alone appropriated the place of privilege that was available to all. It was *love* that drew John into a deeper intimacy with Jesus than the other apostles. Jesus loved them all, but John alone appropriated the title "the disciple whom Jesus loved." If Jesus loved John more, it was because John loved Him more. Mutual love and confidence are the keys to intimacy.

It would seem that admission to the inner circle of deepening intimacy with God is the outcome of *deep desire*. Only those who count such intimacy a prize worth sacrificing anything else for, are likely to attain it. If other intimacies are more desirable to us, we will not gain entry to that circle.

The place on Jesus' breast is still vacant, and open to any who are willing to pay the price of deepening intimacy. We are now, and we will be in the future, only as intimate with God as we really choose to be.

Notes

1. J. I. Packer, *Knowing God* (London: Hodder & Stoughton, 1973), p. 41.
2. J. Elder Cumming, *Keswick Week 1906* (London: Marshalls, 1906), p. 22.

What is worship? Worship is to feel in your heart and express in some appropriate manner a humbling but delightful sense of admiring awe and astonished wonder and overpowering love in the presence of that most ancient Mystery, that Majesty which philosophers call the First Cause, but which we call Our Father Which Art in Heaven. [1]

A. W. Tozer

2

Intimacy Is Nourished by Worship

Exodus 34:5-8, 29-30

In the act of worship, God communicates His presence to His people. That is borne out by the experience of Dr. R. A. Torrey, who girdled the globe with his revival-kindling evangelistic missions. He testified that a transformation came into his experience when he learned not only to give thanks and make petition, but also to worship—asking nothing from God, occupied and satisfied with Him alone. In that new experience, he realized a new intimacy with God.

As His disciples heard the Master pray, they could not help but discern the depth of intimacy that existed between Him and His Father. Aspiration after a similar experience was kindled in their hearts, and they asked Him, "Lord, teach us to pray just as John also taught his disciples" (Luke 11:1). He gladly responded, for was not this the very road along which He had been leading them?

In replying to their request, Jesus said, "When you pray, say: *'Father'* (Luke 11:2, italics added). A sense of the true fatherhood of God in all the richness of that relationship cannot but kindle worship—the loving ascription of praise to God for all that He is, both in His person and providence.

Jesus thus impressed upon His students the important principle that in prayer God must occupy the supreme place, not we ourselves, or even our urgent needs. What a wealth of meaning was compressed into that single word, "Father," as it fell from the lips of Jesus. If God is not accorded the chief place in our prayer life, our prayers will be tepid and pallid. It is significant that in the pattern prayer, it is half completed before Jesus instructed them to mention their own personal needs. When God is given His rightful place, faith will be stimulated.

The idea of worship is endemic in the human race, for man is essentially a worshiping being. But the term as commonly used seldom conveys its true scriptural content. Its old English form, "worthship," provides an interesting sidelight on its meaning. It implies worthiness on the part of the one who receives it.

The ascription of praise to the Lamb in the midst of the throne in Revelation 5:12-14 is an example of the purest worship:

> Worthy is the Lamb that was slain to receive power and riches and wisdom and might and honor and glory and blessing.
>
> To Him who sits on the throne, and to the Lamb, be blessing and honor and glory and dominion forever and ever.
> And the elders fell down and worshiped.

The word "worship" derives from a word meaning "to prostrate oneself, to bow down." It is used of a dog fawning before its master. As we use it, it is "the act of paying reverence and honor to God." When we pray, "Hallowed be Thy name," we are worshiping Him. It conjures up in our minds all that that name connotes.

When God revealed Himself to Moses on Mount Sinai, it was through His name: "And the LORD descended in the cloud and stood there with him. . . . Then the LORD . . . proclaimed, 'The LORD, the LORD God, compassionate and gracious, slow to anger, and abounding in loving-kindness and truth; who keeps loving-kindness for thousands, who forgives iniquity, transgression and sin; yet He will by no means leave the guilty unpunished" (Exod. 34:5-7).

But it is in the area of worship that many evangelicals are most deficient, as John R. W. Stott writes.

> We evangelicals do not know much about worship. Evangelism is our specialty, not worship. We have little sense of the greatness of Almighty God. We tend to be cocky, flippant, and proud. And our worship services are often ill-prepared, slovenly, mechanical, perfunctory and dull. . . . Much of our public worship is ritual without reality, form without power, religion without God.[2]

Endless material for worship is enshrined in divine revelation, for worship is simply the adoring contemplation of God as He has been pleased to reveal Himself in His Son and in the Scriptures, especially in the Psalms, the inspired book of prayer.

Few have mastered the art of worship as did F. W. Faber. To read some of his hymns and poems is a rare experience of worship.

> How wonderful, how beautiful
> The sight of Thee must be,
> Thine endless wisdom, boundless power
> And awful purity.
> O how I fear Thee, living God,
> With deepest, tenderest fears,
> And worship Thee with trembling hope
> And penitential tears.

Hear him again as he is lost in adoration:

> Only to sit and think of God,
> Oh, what joy it is!
> To think the thought, to breathe the Name,
> Earth has no higher bliss!

Father of Jesus, love's Reward,
What rapture will it be,
Prostrate before Thy throne to lie
And gaze, and gaze on Thee.

WORSHIP AND LOVE

Worship flows from love. Where love is meager, worship will
be scant. Where love is deep, worship will overflow. As Paul
wrote his letters, his contemplation of the love and glory of
God would spontaneously cause his heart to overflow in
worship and doxology.

But there can be an element of selfishness even in love.
True, we should worship God for the great things He has
done for us, but our worship reaches a much higher level
when we worship Him simply and solely for what He is, for
the excellences and perfections of His being.

Thomas Goodwin, the Puritan, said, "I have known men
who came to God for nothing else but just to come to Him,
they so loved Him. They scorned to soil Him and themselves
with any other errand than just purely to be alone with Him
in His presence." We might say with some justification that
that is a little extreme, but it betokens an intimacy with God
and desire for fellowship with Him that we might well covet.

Worship is the loving ascription of praise to God, for what
He is in Himself and in His providential dealings. It is the
bowing of our innermost spirit before Him in deepest humility and reverence.

The essence of worship is illustrated in the return of Scipio
Africanus from the conquest of his enemies. As he went, he
scattered the largess of the victor to the crowds that lined the
way. Some were stirred to gratitude by his liberality; some
because he had rolled away from their homes the fear of the
invading army; still others, forgetful of their personal bene-
fits, praised the qualities of the victor—his courage, re-
sourcefulness, liberality. It was in that last group that the
highest element of worship was present.

WORSHIP CAN BE WORDLESS

David adjured his soul: "My soul, wait in silence for God only" (Psalm 62:5). The deepest feelings often cannot find adequate expression in words. Between intimate friends there can be comfortable silences. There are times when words are unnecessary, or even an intrusion. So in our communication with God. Sometimes we are awed into silence in the presence of the Eternal.

A SINGLE WORD CAN ENSHRINE A WEALTH OF WORSHIP

When the disconsolate Mary was weeping outside the empty tomb, she turned and saw Jesus but did not recognize Him until "Jesus said to her, 'Mary!' She turned and said to Him in Hebrew, 'Rabboni!' (John 20:16) In that single word was compressed all the passionate love and reverent worship of a devoted friend and follower.

How Worship May Be Stimulated

Intimacy with God will inevitably fan the flame of desire to know Him better, so that we may worship Him more worthily. How can we stimulate and gratify that desire?

God has granted a glorious, although only partial, revelation of Himself in the wonders of His creation. "The heavens are telling of the glory of God;" wrote David. "And their expanse is declaring the work of His hands" (Psalm 19:1). From His inconceivably vast universe, we can learn something of His majesty, infinite power and wisdom, beauty and orderliness.

> The heavens declare Thy glory, Lord,
>   In every star Thy wisdom shines;
> But when our eyes behold Thy Word,
>   We read Thy name in fairer lines.
>
> Isaac Watts

But the heavens do not declare the mercy and love of God. Only in the face of Jesus Christ do we see the full blaze of the divine glory, for "it was the Father's good pleasure for all the fulness to dwell in Him" (Col. 1:19). No worship that ignores Christ is acceptable to God, for it is only through Him that we can know and have access to the Father.

> In Thee most perfectly expressed,
>   The Father's glories shine,
> Of the full deity possessed,
>   Eternally divine.
> Worthy, O Lamb of God art Thou,
> That every knee to Thee should bow.
>
> Josiah Conder

The question then arises: How can I get to know better and more intimately the Christ who reveals the Father? Primarily through the Scriptures as they are illuminated by the inspiring Holy Spirit. They are rich with material to feed and stimulate worship and adoration. The Scriptures are the only tangible way of knowing Him, as Jesus Himself indicated: "You search the Scriptures, because you think that in them you have eternal life; and it is these that bear witness of Me" (John 5:39).

In the Bible, we have the full and adequate revelation of the vast scope of the divine nature. Great tracts of truth await our exploration. Great themes—God's sovereignty, truth, holiness, wisdom, love, faithfulness, patience, mercy—illumined and made relevant to us by the Holy Spirit, will feed the flame of our worship.

The devotional use of a good hymn book, especially the sections that deal with the Person and work of the members of the Trinity, will prove a great aid to a deeper, more intimate knowledge of God. Not all of us find it easy to express our deepest feelings or to utter our love to God. When we are in the place of prayer, we are painfully conscious of the poverty of our thoughts of God and the paucity of words in which to express them. God has given the church gifted hymn writers to help His less gifted children pour out their worship and praise, and we can take their words and make them our own. Many of the church's great hymns are the nearest thing to divine inspiration.

We should, however, beware of conceiving of worship as being confined solely to the realm of thought, for in Scripture it is linked with service. "YOU SHALL WORSHIP THE LORD YOUR GOD, AND SERVE HIM ONLY," were our Lord's words to Satan (Matt. 4:10). We should not separate what God has joined. Worship is no substitute for service, nor is service a substitute for worship. But true worship must always be expressed in loving service.

Notes

1. D. J. Fant, *A. W. Tozer* (Harrisburg: Christian Publications, 1964), p. 90.
2. John R. W. Stott, "Worship," *Christianity Today,* March 1979, p. 37.

" 'To whom will you compare Me? Or who is My equal?' says the Holy One" (Isa. 40:25, NIV). This question rebukes **wrong thoughts about God.** *"Your thoughts of God are too human,"* *said Luther to Erasmus. This is where most of us go astray. Our thoughts of God are not great enough; we fail to reckon with the reality of His limitless wisdom and power. Because we ourselves are limited and weak, we imagine that at some points God is too, and find it hard to believe that He is not.* [1]

J. I. Packer

3

Intimacy Magnifies God's Greatness

Isaiah 40

The closer we draw to God, the more we are awed by His greatness and majesty. The prophet Isaiah recorded the effect the vision of the transcendent God had upon him: "Woe is me, for I am ruined! Because I am a man of unclean lips . . . for my eyes have seen the King, the LORD of hosts" (6:5). The Lord graciously cleansed him, drew him into a closer intimacy than he had ever before experienced, and entrusted him with amazing insight into the divine character.

In the latter half of his prophecy, Isaiah depicted to the discouraged exiles a God who is incredibly great and majestic, but who yearns over His people and tenderly woos them back into fellowship with Himself.

Isaiah 40 has, with justification, been termed one of the noblest pieces of prose in the English language. No passage of Scripture surpasses it in sublimity of thought or felicity of expression. It combines in a unique way a simplicity and majesty that compels us to realize the inadequacy of our conception of God. Its theme, the awesome transcendence and tender love of God, is worthily expressed in the Swedish hymn:

Oh Lord my God, when I in awesome wonder,
    Consider all the worlds* Thy hands have made,
I see the stars, I hear the rolling * thunder,
    Thy power throughout the universe displayed:
Then sings my soul, my Savior God to Thee,
    How great Thou art!

                                        Stuart K. Hine

The first section of the chapter presents to the exiled Jewish nation a tenderhearted God.

TENDER IN HIS ATTITUDES—40:1-11

In dramatic yet tender language, the prophet brought God's message to His chastened people. "Comfort, O comfort My people,' says your God. 'Speak kindly to Jerusalem' " (vv. 1-2). That wooing note of love must have evoked a warm response in the heart of exiles pining for their homeland.

AN ASSURANCE OF PARDON (40:2)

First he told them that though the nation's sin had been black, it had been pardoned; and her warfare, or hard service, had ended. The divine discipline had achieved its purpose, and the penalty of her iniquity had been accepted as paid off. Now the grace of God could be freely expressed toward her.

THE NECESSITY FOR PREPARATION (40:3-4)

Next the prophet stressed what they must do if the glory of God was again to be revealed in their midst. "Make smooth in the desert a highway for our God." In the East, a victorious general, returning from his conquest, was accorded the victor's triumph. History records titanic feats of engineering in making perfect roads through the trackless desert for the

---

*Author's original words are "works" and "mighty." Copyright 1953, 1955 by Manna Music, Inc., 2111 Kenmere Ave., Burbank, CA 91504. International copyright secured. All rights reserved. Used by permission.

conquering hero. Every low place was filled, every high place reduced, every uneven place leveled, every rough place smoothed so that the conqueror might enjoy unimpeded progress.

John the Baptist referred to that custom when describing his function as forerunner of the Messiah (Matt. 3:3). But it also enshrines an important and contemporary spiritual principle. If God is to reveal Himself in special blessing to His people, there must be prior spiritual preparation. John's task was to create in the nation such a sense of sin and repentance as would make it right and possible for the Holy Spirit to work in power among them.

So it must be among God's people today. Anything crooked in the life must be straightened, any stumbling blocks removed. Low levels of spiritual living must be raised, and rough elements of character polished. Areas of neglect must be remedied, and relationships adjusted. This is something for which we alone are responsible, but the Holy Spirit will cooperate with us to this end.

A REVELATION OF THE GLORY OF GOD (40:5-9)

Once preparation had been made, God's people could expect Him to reveal His glory. The sequence is natural. Cleanness of heart brings clearness of vision. Only the pure in heart see God. New vision follows new adjustment: "Then the glory of the LORD will be revealed, and all flesh will see it together; for the mouth of the LORD has spoken" (v. 5). But in contrast to the glory of God, Isaiah set the frailty and transience of man (vv. 6-7). Compared with the permanence and changelessness of God and His Word (v. 8), man is just like withering grass.

GOD IS THE ONE WHO IS INFINITELY STRONG (40:10-11)

"Behold, the LORD GOD will come with might, with His arm ruling for Him" (v. 10). His rule of the nation would be inflexibly just, yet *considerately tender.* "Like a shepherd He will tend His flock, in His arm He will gather the lambs, and carry them in His bosom; He will gently lead the nursing ewes" (v. 11).

The One who leads His people is terrible in His might, yet tender in His attitudes. Though Judge and Ruler of the universe, He tenderly leads His flock in green pastures and by still waters. His mighty arm gathers the tired lambs to His bosom. He rests them in the heat of the day. He adapts His pace to the weakest of His flock. Surely, "the heart of the Eternal is most wonderfully kind."

A great deal of teaching in Scripture is by paradox, as in this passage. It is difficult to hold in the mind at the same time the contrasting qualities of goodness and severity, of loftiness and lowliness, of humility and majesty. Yet those are all ascribed to God here and elsewhere. "No attribute of God is in conflict with another. God is never at cross-purposes with Himself," wrote A. W. Tozer.[2]

The second portion of the chapter reveals God's attributes.

TRANSCENDENT IN HIS ATTRIBUTES—40:12-28

Isaiah strengthened his message of comfort to the exiles with bracing and stimulating thoughts of the attributes of the eternal God. In graphic language, he portrayed some of the elements of the divine character.

HE IS SELF-SUFFICIENT (40:12-14)

God needs neither the advice nor the aid of man in running His universe. God is necessary to man, but man is not necessary to God. The prophet asked, "Who has measured the waters in the hollow of His hand, and marked off the heavens by the span. . . . Who has directed the Spirit of the LORD, or as His counselor has informed Him? With whom did He consult and who gave Him understanding?" (40:12-14)

Israel's God needed no one to pity or defend Him. "A God who must be defended is one who can help us only while someone is helping Him."[3] Man's sin may delay the fulfilment of God's eternal purpose, but it cannot defeat it. There are no surprises for God, nor does He have to resort to emergency action.

HE IS OMNIPOTENT (40:12)

In verse 12, Isaiah compared God to a workman using weights and measures. From that figure, he adduced a sublime conception of God. He saw the vast oceans over which we sail week after week as but a drop in the hand of the Infinite. Mighty mountains are like specks of dust in His scales. So far-reaching are His fingers in their span, that they encompass the heavens. So powerful are His arms, that they effortlessly hold the scales in which lie the loftiest mountains. He is the mighty God who will deliver Israel.

> In all our Maker's grand designs
> Omnipotence with wisdom shines;
> His works, through all this wondrous frame,
> Declare the glory of His name.
>
> Thomas Blacklock

HE IS OMNISCIENT (40:13-14, 28)

God needs no assistance from any external source. He needs no one with whom to consult, for His wisdom is inexhaustible. His knowledge is self-derived. "Who . . . taught Him knowledge, and informed Him of the way of understanding?" He knows all and foresees all. He always knows what His next move will be. His wisdom is unsearchable.

HE IS INCOMPARABLE (40:18, 25)

"To whom then will you liken God?" asks the prophet. "Or what likeness will you compare with Him?" He is solitary and unique in every aspect of His nature. He is not a mere magnified man, so what utter folly to try to make similitudes of the infinite God in wood or metal or stone! (vv. 19-20) Inert material substances could never express the majesty and glory of God.

HE IS SOVEREIGN (40:15, 17, 23)

For centuries the surrounding nations had been ravaging Israel. Now the prophet invited them to see those nations in true perspective. "Behold, the nations are like a drop from a bucket, and are regarded as a speck of dust on the scales. . . . All the nations are as nothing before Him, they are regarded by Him as less than nothing and meaningless."

The drop of water does not increase the burden of the one who carries it, nor does the speck of dust weigh down the scales. In His sovereign power God "lifts up the islands like fine dust."

Such a conception would hardly be acceptable to a Caesar, a Napoleon, a Hitler, a Stalin, an Idi Amin! But in contrast to the infinite and eternal One, earthly rulers are nothing and reduced to meaninglessness.

> In Thy sovereignty rejoicing,
> We Thy children bow and praise,
> For we know that kind and loving,
> Just and true are all Thy ways.
> While Thy heart of sovereign mercy,
> And Thy arm of sovereign might,
> For our great and strong salvation
> In Thy sovereign grace unite.
>
> Frances Ridley Havergal

HE IS TRANSCENDENT (40:22-24)

The picture is now transferred from earth to sky. God is represented as sitting enthroned above earth's vault, "above the circle of the earth." Such a conception is more easily intelligible to our generation than it would have been in ancient times. Our spacemen, from their vantage point above the earth, were able to see whole continents. From His elevated throne, God sees and controls the whole universe.

> Lord of all being, throned afar,
> Thy glory flames from sun and star;

> Center and soul of every sphere,
> Yet to each loving heart how near!
>
> Oliver Wendell Holmes

Creating the innumerable heavenly galaxies cost God no more effort than hanging a tent curtain: "Who stretches out the heavens like a curtain and spreads them out like a tent to dwell in." Small wonder that to Him earth's "inhabitants are like grasshoppers." With a God as great as that, why should His people fear what earth's puny potentates could do? "He merely blows on them, and they wither."

HE IS ETERNAL (40:26, 28)

The scene shifts once again, and the heavens are represented as a battlefield. As Supreme Commander, God gathers the starry host as a general who knows all his men by name and by sight. "He calls them all by name . . . not one of them is missing." Under His banner and providential care they are kept safe.

We are prisoners of time and space, tied to clock and calendar, scrabbling for dollars and cents, limited by feet and yards. But the uncreated God transcends all time and space. He is everlasting and moves through eternity with unhurried tread, for He is "the high and exalted One who lives forever, whose name is Holy" (Isa. 57:15).

> Thou Knowest not how I uphold
>   The little thou dost scan;
> And how much less canst thou unfold
>   My universal plan.
> Where all thy mind can grasp of space
>   Is but a grain of sand—
> The time thy boldest thought can trace
>   One ripple on the strand.
>
> Frances Ridley Havergal

HE IS IMMUTABLE (40:28)

"The Everlasting God, the LORD . . . does not become weary

or tired." He is eternally the same. "THE HEAVENS ARE THE WORKS OF THY HANDS; THEY WILL PERISH, BUT THOU REMAINEST; AND THEY ALL WILL BECOME OLD AS A GARMENT, . . . AS A GARMENT THEY WILL ALSO BE CHANGED. BUT THOU ART THE SAME AND THY YEARS WILL NOT COME TO AN END" (Heb. 1:10-12). Our God is majestic in His eternal unchangeableness. It is a comforting thought that that attribute of God is coupled in Scripture, not with His judgment merely, but with His grace and mercy. "I, the LORD, do not change; therefore you, O sons of Jacob, are not consumed" (Mal. 3:6).

> Fountain of being! Source of Good!
> Immutable Thou dost remain!
> Nor can the shadow of a change
> Obscure the glories of Thy reign.
> (George) Walker's Collection

THE APPROPRIATE RESPONSE

What adequate and worthy response can we make to a God so great, so holy, so transcendent?

"Even Lebanon is not enough to burn, nor its beasts enough for a burnt offering" (Isa. 40:16). To use all the cedars of Lebanon to kindle an altar fire to consume all the cattle on its slopes, would be no extravagance. Our debt to Him is so great that no conceivable sacrifice would be too great to make for Him, since sacrifice is "the ecstasy of giving the best we have to the One we love the most."

Notes

1. J. I. Packer, *Knowing God* (London: Hodder & Stoughton, 1973), p. 94.
2. A. W. Tozer, *Knowledge of the Holy* (Harrisburg: Christian Publications, 1961), p. 95.
3. Ibid., p. 41.

The threefold provision which God has made against sin embraces cleansing, expiation and an Advocate. Admission into fellowship, in spite of sins discovered and confessed, is the essence of forgiveness, which has to do with the personal relationship which sin has broken. Welcome replaces banishment, favor cancels condemnation—the flaming sword is lowered—and we have access by faith, into this grace wherein we stand.[1]

R. E. O. White

4

Intimacy Is Preceded by Cleansing

1 John 1:8—2:2

"Do two walk together unless they have agreed to do so?" the prophet Amos inquired (Amos 3:3, NIV). Of course not! Then how is it possible for a holy God to have intimate fellowship with sinful and sometimes sinning men and women? The question will arise at once in the thoughtful mind.

Scripture is realistic in its treatment of sin, whether in the believer or unbeliever. It recognizes that sin is a continuing problem, even for the believer. He is not forever done with sin when he is converted, because he never gets beyond the reach of temptation. True, he has experienced the joy of forgiveness. He revels in the assurance that his guilt has been removed, but he is nowhere promised exemption from the lure of temptation or the possibility of sinning.

Has the reader never been shocked by the unexpected revival of old sins, or at sudden attacks of the devil who has no respect for even our holiest hours? And those are only surface manifestations. What lies hidden in the depths of our subconscious mind—below the level of consciousness? The Master Psychologist gave His diagnosis: "From within, out of the heart of men, proceed the evil thoughts and fornications, thefts, murders, adulteries." (Mark 7:21). Then how is it possible for a God who hates sin and requires purity, to continue having dealings with a sin-prone believer, to say nothing of permitting a deepening intimacy? The answer is that in the multi-faceted death of His Son, provision is made for a cleansing so deep, so radical, so continuous that a believer can walk with God in unbroken communion and deepening fellowship. Only the pure in heart can have the vision of God, and, for that, cleansing is essential.

Even in Old Testament times, "Enoch walked with God" in a fellowship so close that the Lord took him straight to heaven without experiencing death (Heb. 11:5). He cultivated a deepening intimacy with God, not on an occasional stroll, but in a walk that covered three hundred years, and that in a godless environment.

God did not walk in the direction Enoch was going. Enoch had to make a break with his godless contemporaries and walk in the direction God was going. And God always moves along the highway of holiness. Had Enoch not fully accepted God's standards and will, his walk would have been a very short one. God and Enoch found in each other mutually congenial company.

If such a close and growing intimacy was possible in the dawn of history, and before the triumph of the cross, how much more should it be possible now.

Scripture is clear that upon believing, we are justified from all things (Acts 13:39). Our sins are forgiven and remembered no more (Heb. 8:12). Because our guilt and penalty were borne by Jesus on the cross, we will never come into judgment for them. But Christians *do* sin after conversion. For such sins, there is forgiveness through the blood of Christ (1 John 1:7). That forgiveness is granted in response to true repentance and confession (1:9).

With that background, let us consider 1 John, chapter 1.

SINS AND SIN

John differentiates between "sin" and "sins." Those words occur four times. The underlying teaching is that "sins"—individual acts of sin—are the manifestation of "sin"—the outcropping of a sinful nature. Any cleansing that will fit us for growing intimacy with God must deal with both aspects, the conscious and the subconscious. Here John assures us that such a provision has been made.

ONLY GOD IS WITHOUT SIN

"God is light, and in Him there is no darkness at all" (1 John 1:5). God cannot sin or be tempted with evil (James 1:13); this fact imparts moral stability to the universe. Because God cannot lie, all His undertakings are dependable.

ALL BELIEVERS HAVE SINNED

"If we say that we have not sinned, we make Him a liar" (1 John 1:10). Some, who believe in the total eradication of the sinful nature upon sanctification, take this verse to refer to sins before conversion. But Scripture nowhere indicates that it is impossible to sin after conversion.

ALL CHRISTIANS HAVE SIN

As if to answer this very objection to sinlessness, John specifically states, "If we say that we have no sin, we are deceiving ourselves" (1 John 1:8). Here the reference is not to specific acts of sin but to the sinful nature. Paul was under no illusions on that point. "I know that nothing good dwells in me" (Rom. 7:18). All believers have a sinful nature, transmitted from Adam, by natural birth. All Christians have a new nature, implanted by the Holy Spirit, and that opens the way for a new possibility.

BELIEVERS SHOULD NOT AND NEED NOT HABITUALLY SIN

"My little children, I am writing these things to you that you may not sin" (1 John. 2:1). Because of our Lord's victory on Calvary and the descent of the Holy Spirit, the believer is no longer under the pressure of the necessity to sin. He will be tempted, but he need not yield, because a new law, stronger than the downward pull of sin, has been brought into operation. "For the law of the Spirit of life in Christ Jesus has set you free from the law of sin and of death" (Rom. 8:2). This means that the believer need no longer live in conscious, willful sin.

John assures us that "no one who abides in Him sins" (1 John 3:6). So long as we are abiding in Christ, we are not sinning. So long as we walk in the Spirit, we need not fulfil the desires of the flesh (Gal. 5:16). Instead, we will produce the fruit of the Spirit (5:22-23).

BUT BELIEVERS MAY, AND DO, SIN

Sometimes believers sin because of an unwelcome carry-over from the former life. "If anyone sins . . ." (1 John 2:1). John took a realistic view of the subtlety of sin and the frailty of human nature. But for such sin, God has graciously made provision in advance. "We have an Advocate with the Father, Jesus Christ the righteous; and He Himself is the propitiation for our sins. . . ." (2:1-2).

His salvation has made full provision for every contingency.

There was a way back even for the adulterer and murderer David. Peter did not forfeit his place in the apostolate because he denied his Lord. But in each case there was deep repentance and real cleansing.

The gracious provision of a divine Advocate to plead our cause is not in order to encourage us to keep on sinning. John specifically said he was writing that we may not sin, but to save us from despair when we have sinned.

THE DIVINE REMEDY MEETS EVERY ASPECT OF OUR NEED

"He Himself is the propitiation for our sins." God's righteous anger is appeased and His holiness vindicated by the sacrifice of Christ, who is the propitiation for our sins.

So far as our *standing before God* is concerned, the blood of Christ answers for all our sins, and He Himself pleads our cause.

Amintas was convicted of crimes against the Roman state and was being tried for treason. Hearing of his plight, his elder brother Aeschylus, who had lost an arm in the service of his country, hastened to the court. Bursting into the room, he lifted his arm stump, and, catching the eye of the judge, he said, "Amintas is guilty, but for Aeschylus' sake, he shall go free." The judge acquitted him. Even so our Intercessor presents the tokens of His sufferings, and the Judge says of us, "They are guilty, but for My Son's sake, they shall go free."

> Five bleeding wounds He bears,
>   Received on Calvary;
> They pour effectual prayers,
>   They strongly plead for me
> Forgive him, O forgive, they cry,
>   Nor let that ransomed sinner die.
>
> Charles Wesley

In our daily walk, it is painfully true that sin breaks our fellowship with God, dissipates our joy in God, and nullifies our witness for God, but there is a way back—"if we confess our sins" (1 John 1:9).

> There is a common and dangerous tendency among us to "cover" our sins. We may go to church and join in the general confession, and in our private prayers say we are sorry for our sins. But our words have a hollow sound. Our confession is largely a formality. We know little of the uncomfortable discipline of confessing and forsaking our sins, and so finding mercy.[2]

It is comparatively easy to confess our *sinfulness* and admit that we are "miserable sinners." But to confess honestly to *specific sins* is more difficult. What is implied in such confession? Since all sin is essentially rebellion against God, no sin is trivial. It is not sufficient merely to say, "I am sorry."

We must take the attitude, "This sin I am confessing is *wrong*, and it must go." It is not mere regret at being found out, but involves a change of mind that results in a change of action. The word "confess" means "to say the same thing." When we confess any sin, it means that we are agreeing with what God says about it, and taking the attitude toward it that He does.

THE EXTENT OF CONFESSION

In order to restore right relationships, we may need to confess to man as well as to God, for we cannot be right with God and wrong with man.

The sincerity of our confession may need to be evidenced by *restitution*. Apology may need to be made, a quarrel settled, a debt paid, a relationship terminated, if we are to enjoy renewed fellowship with God and man.

Here there arises the question of what we should confess and to whom we should confess it.

As all sin is against God, obviously we should confess to Him every sin of which we are conscious, and we should do it without delay, as soon as we realize we have sinned. Some sins are against God alone, but others are against our fellow men, and thus require confession to them.

The scriptural principle involved would seem to be that the confession should be coextensive with the sin. Where the sin is against God alone, the sin need be confessed only to God. There may sometimes be therapeutic value in sharing our problem with another trusted friend, but there is no necessity to do so.

Where the sin is against a fellow man, the sin should be confessed to the one who has been injured by our sin, and need be confessed to no other. There is nothing to be gained merely by giving someone else, who is not involved, a knowledge of your sin.

Where the sin is against a church or group, the sin should be confessed to the church or group in an appropriate manner, probably to the leader, who could decide what action, if any, should be taken.

What about public confession? There may be cases where that is called for, but they would be rare. Meetings at which there is promiscuous public confession of personal sins should not be encouraged, as they are often definitely harmful.

There are, however, occasions, especially during times of revival, when, under the pressure of the Holy Spirit, the person can find relief only by confessing specific sins in prayer, and the writer has seen that on several occasions. But it has always been accompanied with deep humility and brokenness. Anything that savors of exhibitionism or prurient interest should be abjured.

THE EXTENT OF THE CLEANSING

> If we confess our *sins*, He . . . [will] . . . cleanse us from *all unrighteousness* (1 John 1:9, italics added).

There is no sin so bad that it is impossible for the sinner to be cleansed from the guilt and pollution that would forbid continuing intimacy with God. Sins of thought, desire, motive, and imagination, as well as sins of action, can all be washed away in the cleansing tide. When the Holy Spirit applies the virtue of the blood of Christ to our hearts, it cleanses, sterilizes, disinfects, and makes us "whiter than snow." Memory can be cleansed and conscience purified. "How much more will the blood of Christ . . . cleanse your conscience." (Heb. 9:14).

Because God is faithful, He cannot deny Himself. Because He is just, He must be true to what His Son achieved on the cross.

THE DURATION OF THE CLEANSING

If we walk in the light . . . the blood of Jesus His Son cleanses us from all sin (1 John 1:7).

> Walk in the light and sin abhorred,
> Shall not defile again;
> The blood of Jesus Christ the Lord
> Shall cleanse from every stain.
>
> Charles Wesley

To walk in unbroken intimacy with God requires an unceasing cleansing, not only from the defilement of individual acts of sin, but also from the pollution of our sinful natures. Verse 7 assures us that as we walk in obedience to the light God gives, the blood of Christ will deal with the subconscious as well as the conscious. It cleanses from every aspect of sin. We can never get beyond the need or the reach of the blood of Christ, and the tense of the verb "cleanseth"—keeps on cleansing—assures us that despite a continuing tendency to sin, we can revel in the continuing cleanness effected by the divine sacrifice.

How may that cleansing be experienced? By faith alone. God has assured us of the facts. It remains for us personally to believe and appropriate the glorious reality that God both forgives the outward act of sin and cleanses us from its inward defilement.

> Precious, precious blood of Jesus,
> Shed on Calvary,
> I believe it, I receive it
> 'Tis for me.

Notes

1. R. E. O. White, *An Open Letter to Evangelicals* (London: Paternoster, 1964), p. 42.
2. John R. W. Stott, *Confess Your Sins*, (Waco, Texas: Word, 1974), p. 15.

The Chronicler omits all reference to this terrible blot on David's life. The older record sets down each item without extenuation or excuse. The gain for all penitents would so much outweigh the loss to the credit of the man after God's own heart. These chapters have been trodden by myriads who, having well nigh lost themselves in the same dark labyrinth of sin, have discovered the glimmer of light by which the soul may pass back into the day. "Thy sins which are many are forgiven thee; go in peace." [1]

F. B. Meyer

5

Intimacy Can Be Forfeited

2 Samuel 11:1-17

In His letter to the church at Ephesus, our Lord paid glowing tribute to their orthodoxy and patient endurance, but He uttered one lament: "But I have this against you, that you have left your first love. Remember therefore from where you have fallen" (Rev. 2:4-5). Had they been so busy doing good works and hating the Nicolaitans that they had stopped loving Christ? Had their love been stifled by their activity? At first thought, that does not seem very serious, but to lose his wife's love is not a small thing to a husband. The Lord considered the defect so serious that unless the Ephesians repented, their witness would be destroyed.

The danger of falling out of love with Christ is no less present in our times, and it occasions our Lord as much grief now as then. Intimacy with God is a fragile thing that must be carefully guarded.

M. Basilea Schlink tells of her own experience of waning love:

> I came to see that my relationship to my Lord Jesus Christ, with the passing years had eroded away, something like a marriage gone humdrum. What did I do when I found a little pocket of spare time, on a Sunday or a holiday? I couldn't wait

to get together with other people—people I liked, people with whom I had something in common—so that we could share ideas and experiences. Or I read a stimulating book. Or I went out to enjoy nature. I even plunged further into my work, doing things that I normally didn't have time for. But to go to Jesus—to give Him first claim on my spare time, that I did not do.[2]

Few Bible saints experienced and expressed so deep an intimacy with God as David. His psalms are studded with expressions of worship and devotion that betoken an exceptionally close walk with God. That walk was maintained even in the midst of constant peril and adversity. Time and again, when surrounded by enemies and discouraged in heart, his confidence in God enabled him to break through the forbidding clouds and again enjoy the sunshine of God's presence.

On experiencing deliverance from the hands of Saul, he sang this song of praise and devotion, which was typical of his outbursts of love and loyalty to his God.

I love Thee, O LORD, my strength.
The LORD is my rock and my fortress and my deliverer,
My God, my rock, in whom I take refuge;
My shield and the horn of my salvation, my stronghold.
I call upon the Lord, who is worthy to be praised,
And I am saved from my enemies.

(Psalm 18:1-3)

The tragedy is that in an unguarded moment the man whom Scripture describes as "a man after [God's] heart" (Acts 13:22), forfeited that treasured intimacy and went out into the dark, an adulterer and a murderer. To us, such a sudden and steep transition seems almost unbelievable, but that is only because we have not yet discovered the dark depths and intricacies of our own hearts.

The fatal fall occurred at "the time when kings go out to battle" (2 Sam. 11:1). His rightful place was at the head of his armies, but he neglected his duty in favor of an unduly prolonged siesta: "Now when evening came David arose from his bed" (11:2). While walking on the roof of his house, David saw a very beautiful woman bathing. His repeated look kindled lust in his heart, and, in one fatal moment, he forfeited his intimacy with God. For a momentary gratification, he sacrificed fellowship with God.

That would have been serious enough, but the man of God descended to even lower depths. In order to cover up his sin, he treacherously plotted and engineered the death of one of his most loyal subjects—the husband of the woman he had seduced. That dark stain is a warning to people in all ages of the possibility of defection in mature years. In a moment, it is possible to sully the achievements of a lifetime. Church history is strewn with stories of similar tragedies. Could David have foreseen the bitter fruit that would spring from his lustful look, he would sooner have lost his right hand than yield to the allurement of the flesh.

A COMPREHENSIVE SIN

Not only did his sin leave an indelible blot on his own life, but it involved his family and his nation as well. None of us sins in isolation. Worse than all, he wantonly forfeited the smile of God. Some scholars believe that the incident marked the beginning of the disintegration of the nation of Israel. David was soon to reap in his own family the tragic harvest he had sown.

> No action, whether foul or fair,
> Is ever done, but it leaves somewhere
> A record written by fingers ghostly,
> As a blessing or a curse, and mostly
> In the greater weakness or greater strength
> Of the acts which follow it: till at length
> The wrongs of ages are redressed,
> And the justice of God made manifest.
>
> Henry Wadsworth Longfellow

Reflection on David's fall will reveal its comprehensiveness. Fallout from it polluted an incredibly large area. In committing that sin, he broke every commandment in the Decalogue that refers to man's duty to his neighbor.

He broke the tenth commandment by coveting his neighbor's wife. That led to his breaking the seventh, and committing adultery. In order to break the eighth—stealing what did not belong to him—he broke the sixth and committed murder. He broke the ninth by bearing false witness against his neighbor, and the fifth by bringing dishonor to his parents.

Whatever else the incident teaches us, it makes crystal clear that there is no such thing as a simple sin. Sin is always complex, and its eddies circle far out into the ocean. And all that evil sprang from a lustful look at a time of illegitimate loafing.

How to Handle Failure

When seeking a king for Israel, God sought and found in David a man after His heart (1 Sam. 13:14). A man or woman after God's heart can be recognized by the way in which he or she handles failure. David's repentance and recovery will be studied in more detail in the next chapter, but it should be noted here, first, that he confessed that his sin was primarily against God (Psalm 51:4); and second, that he confessed it brokenly and with bitter tears. His prayers in Psalm 51 are little more than broken sobs, wrung out of him by a profound sorrow and deep repentance.

> O Father, I have sinned! I have done
> The thing I thought I never more should do!
> My days were set before me, light all through;
> But I have made dark—alas, too true!
> And drawn dense clouds between me and my Sun.
>
> Septimus Sutton

When a man after God's heart repents, there is nothing superficial about it. With David, repentance was not mere remorse or regret at being found out, it was deep and radical. If he has been rendered notorious for his sin, he has been made immortal by the quality and sincerity of his repentance.

His repentance formed the basis of restoration to full fellowship with the God whom he had insulted and grieved. The sinning saint was once more admitted into the intimacy with God that he had forfeited.

But although his sin was forgiven and fellowship restored, the temporal consequences could not be averted. As Moral Governor of the universe, God could not tolerantly overlook the wider implications of the king's sin, and the remainder of his life led him through some dark valleys.

DAVID'S HEART WAS RIGHT WITH GOD

Although he failed so grievously, David's fall was not characteristic, but accidental. It was entirely contrary to the tenor of his life. His sins were temporary, not habitual, for his inner attitude to God was basically one of love and loyalty. Through the trauma of that experience he learned, and teaches us, that no failure, however grievous, need be final. To the penitent saint, God is always the God of the second chance.

To the repentant prophet Jonah, "the word of the LORD came . . . the second time" (Jonah 3:1). When the pot was marred in the potter's hand, "he remade it into another vessel as it pleased the potter to make" (Jer. 18:4).

In the answer to his plea, God did restore to David the joy of his salvation and washed him whiter than snow. The old intimacy with God was regained, but was its music now in a minor key?

The evidence that his heart was right with God is seen in the spirit in which he received and reacted to the divine discipline. Like his greater Son, he had to tread the bitter path of rejection. He was rejected by his brothers. Saul treated him like an outlaw and hunted him like a partridge on the mountains. He was rejected by his favorite son, Absalom. He was rejected by the nation and forced into exile—a melancholy experience for one who loved his people so passionately. Yet in it all, he manifested true submission to God and acceptance of His disciplines. His was true spiritual maturity.

It is probably true that no other Bible character experienced so many rapid changes of fortune over so long a period. Because he touched the heights and depths of human experience at so many points, he was uniquely qualified to compose the psalms that have voiced the desires and aspirations, the sighs and sorrows of succeeding generations.

His sufferings produced a sympathy and understanding of human nature that gave him a many-sided appeal to saints in all ages. The Holy Spirit was able to use his remarkable natural gifts and diverse experiences to produce poetry and hymns of deep insight and popular appeal.

> Is it true O Christ in heaven, that the highest
>   suffer the most?
> That the strongest wander furthest and most
>   hopelessly are lost?
> That the mark of rank in nature is capacity
>   for pain?
> That the anguish of the singer makes the sweet
>   ness of the strain?
>
> John Milton

In David's writings, the major chords of worship, praise, and thanksgiving blend with the minor chords of penitence and confession to make heavenly harmony. The lesson for us is that our great God can take even our failures and the adverse experiences of life to give comfort to those in need and to create a beautiful symphony. Such experiences are the price of a ministry.

DAVID'S CAPACITY FOR FRIENDSHIP

The man after God's heart will reflect the attitude of the One who deigned to call frail men His friends. "No longer do I call you slaves; . . . I have called you friends" (John 15:15). David's capacity for friendship was one of the qualities that made him a man after God's heart.

Friendship begets intimacy, and in times of difficulty and danger it is a great strength to have a staunch friend alongside. God gave David that compensation in Jonathan, Saul's son. In their association, those men have given us an example of ideal friendship. We can gain much insight into the character of our fellows by observing the number and quality of their friends. It is still true as an old German quaintly put it, "Birds mit one feather flock mit themselves."

David befriended unfortunates who had no friends and won from them an almost fanatical love and loyalty. His followers in the cave of Adullam were a motley group of outlaws, outcasts, and unemployed. Yet from that unpromising material, he molded an elite and powerful fighting force. Like Jesus, David was the friend of publicans and sinners.

He was a natural leader, possessing charm and charisma that won the love and loyalty of his men. He had only to breathe a wish for a drink from the familiar well at Bethlehem, for his men to risk their lives to obtain it for him. Not only was he a born leader, but he was a loyal, considerate friend to those who threw in their lot with him.

Jonathan's self-effacing friendship with him stands out in sharp relief against the jealousy and perfidy of his father, Saul. It is one of the mysteries of life that such a father should have such a son, in whom malignity and perfidy were displaced by magnanimity and integrity.

David and Jonathan were twin souls—men of similar tastes and interests—and they displayed the same spirit in times of testing. Jonathan's renunciation of his throne in favor of his friend and rival is one of the noblest acts of history. There are some friendships that weaken, but

Jonathan "strengthened David's hands in God." Fortunate is the one who is privileged to enjoy the intimacy of such a friendship.

DAVID'S REACTION TO DISAPPOINTMENT

The man who is on intimate terms with God does not misinterpret His providential dealings, even though he may not understand them. That was true of David, for he accepted his disappointments in a mature way.

He conceived the noble purpose of building a house worthy of his God. It was to be a magnificent edifice, the crowning achievement of his life. But when his scheme was rejected by God because he was a man of bloodshed (2 Sam. 7:1-5, 12-13), though desperately disappointed, he did not sulk or go sour. Instead, he gave his strength and wealth to gathering materials for the house that his son Solomon was to build.

If our ideals are sometimes not realized or our desires thwarted, the incident is very relevant. David was the forerunner of many disappointed men and women whose purpose and motives are accepted by the Lord, but whose actual services may be denied or postponed. Although God did not permit David to build His house, He said to him, "Because it was in your heart to build a house for My name, you did well that it was in your heart" (1 Kings 8:18). The purpose was accepted by God for the deed.

DAVID'S EXERCISE OF RESTRAINT

From the time that Samuel anointed him until he actually reached the throne, David had abundant opportunities to exercise patience and restraint. His fortunes ebbed and flowed with monotonous regularity, yet never once did he petulantly take the reins into his own hands or endeavor to force the premature fulfilment of his promised destiny. David left the timing in God's hands, fully confident that in

God's time he would reach the throne. Intimacy begets trust.

On several occasions, he had opportunity to hasten the denouement, and his men were only too willing to aid and abet him, but he restrained them. They were at a loss to understand his reluctance to seize what appeared to be God-given opportunities to consummate his victories. But David realized that sometimes such opportunities were tests. He gave short shrift to the Amalekite who dared to kill Saul, the Lord's anointed king (2 Sam. 1:13-15).

Izaak Walton's summary of David's life was that he was a man after God's heart because he abounded more in thanksgiving than any other person mentioned in Scripture. He was the thankful man of the Old Testament.

As an old man, he sang a song of thanksgiving and praise that affords a clue to the maturity of his walk with God. In it are these gems:

> As for God, His way is perfect.
> It is God who arms me with strength and makes
>   my way perfect.
> The Word of the Lord is flawless.
> You stoop down to make me great.
>
> (2 Sam. 22:31, 33, 36, NIV)

Notes

1. F. B. Meyer, *David* (London: Morgan & Scott, 1927), p. 171.
2. George Sweeting, *Love Lost and Found* (Chicago: Moody, 1968), p. 133.

Penitent soul! Dare to believe in the instantaneous forgiveness of sins. Thou hast only to utter the confession, to find it interrupted with the outbreak of the Father's love. As soon as the words of penitence leave thy lips, they are met by the hurrying assurances of a love which, whilst it hates sin, has never ceased to yearn over the prodigal. [1]

F. B. Meyer

6

Intimacy Can Be Restored

Psalm 51

If the previous chapter highlights how intimacy with God can be forfeited, Psalm 51 reveals graphically how it can be restored.

The greatest of the seven penitential psalms, it is a poignant and moving piece of autobiography. It is a classic on a sinning man's progress from stubborn impenitence, through deep repentance, to glorious restoration. The language, like the experience it portrays, is contemporary and relevant for every age and race. Who of us has not had occasion to make Psalm 51 our own and to tread with David the path of contrition and restoration?

The title gives the clue to its occasion: "For the choir director. A psalm of David, when Nathan the prophet came to him, after he had gone in to Bathsheba."

Infatuated with the beautiful Bathsheba, the king had fallen into the sordid sin of adultery, which in turn involved him a squalid intrigue that climaxed in the murder of her husband, Uriah. After a period of obstinate refusal to confess his sin (see Psalm 32:3-4), God used the soul-searching charge of Nathan the prophet—"You are the man!"—to bring home the enormity of David's sin, while at the same time displaying His own boundless mercy and grace. "The Lord also has taken away your sin" (2 Sam. 12:7, 13). God never leaves a penitent sinner in the dust.

The psalm is the uninhibited, broken outpouring of a soul overwhelmed with a sense of guilt, the outburst of sincere repentance after a disgraceful, inexcusable episode. And yet it is full of encouragement, for it reveals the heart of God and His attitude toward those who have failed.

We may not have fallen into sins so socially unacceptable as those of David, but are our sins and failures any more acceptable in God's sight? *All* sin ruptures fellowship, destroys intimacy with God, produces a sense of guilt, and involves the sinning person in painful temporal and eternal loss.

David made no attempt to clothe his prayer with flowing rhetoric, for it is simply a series of brokenhearted sobs. He pleaded no extenuating circumstances and attempted no self-vindication. The magnitude of his sin is not toned down, but is freely acknowledged. Hear the broken sobs, expressed in vivid verbs: Have mercy! Cleanse! Blot out! Wash! Purge! Hide Your face from my sins! Create! Do not cast! Renew! Restore! Save! Open my lips!

Here is true confession, free from all sham and insincerity. Examine it in detail.

CONFESSION OF GUILT—51:1-6

The concept behind the Greek word for "confess" is, "to say the same thing," in other words, to admit oneself to be guilty of what one is charged with. When we confess our sin and acknowledge our guilt to God, we agree with Him in His assessment of the seriousness of our sin and take sides with Him against it (Psalm 32:1-5).

A PLEA FOR CLEANSING

David took that ground in Psalm 51, which opens with his prayer, "Be gracious to me, O God" (51:1-2). For David, forgiveness was not sufficient if it left him still with a burden of guilt and sense of defilement. The intolerable weight must be lifted and the pollution removed, so he asked for another boon: *"Blot out* my transgressions."* Erase and obliterate them so completely that not a trace remains, *"Wash me* thoroughly from my iniquity"—so that every stain is bleached. *"Cleanse me* from my sin"—even as the leper was cleansed from his loathsome disease.

> So wash me Thou, without, within,
> Or purge with fire, if that must be;
> No matter how, if only sin
>   Be cleansed by Thee!

Walter C. Smith

The Holy Spirit had worked in the penitent king an acute sense of sin, so acute that no single word was sufficient to express it. He used three words to confess his realization of the sinfulness of his sin—*transgression*, the overstepping and breaking of God's law; *iniquity*, that which is off the straight, morally crooked; *sin*, missing the mark, failing to reach the divine standard and goal. He confessed that he was guilty of sin in all its aspects.

ACKNOWLEDGMENT OF EXCLUSIVE GUILT

"Against Thee, Thee only, I have sinned" (51:4). Under the pressure of the Holy Spirit, David realized that ultimately *all* sin is against God. It insults Him and is rebellion against His sovereignty. He realized, too, that his had not been private sins, for they affected not only himself but the whole nation.

Up until that time his chief thought had been, "How can I cover my tracks?" But now his only concern was, "How ever could I have offered such an insult to a loving and holy God!"

Though God heard his plea and forgave him, David did not escape the social consequences of his fall. But his present concern was not for the results as they would affect him; his sorrow stemmed from a humbling sense of the shame he had brought on the name of his God. Without demur, he accepted the divine verdict on his sin: "So that Thou art justified when Thou dost speak, and blameless when Thou dost judge" (v. 4).

A NEW INSIGHT INTO THE NATURE OF SIN

This attitude enabled David to say, "Behold, I was brought forth in iniquity, and in sin my mother conceived me" (51:5). David was not casting any reflection on his mother, or suggesting that conception is in itself sinful. Rather, he was indicating that he now saw that his outward crimes were only the expression of his inveterately sinful nature. Many years later, David's greater Son revealed their source: "Out of the heart come evil thoughts, murders, adulteries, fornications" (Matt. 15:19). The king was overwhelmed at the depravity of the heart that had dragged him to such depths of degradation.

A FRESH APPRECIATION OF THE DIVINE REQUIREMENTS

That discovery led him to realize: "Behold, Thou dost desire truth in the innermost being" (51:6). Only absolute truth and utter sincerity would avail if he were to get right with the God who is interested in inward purity, not mere outward respectability, and once again enjoy intimacy with Him.

We each have endless capacity for self-deception and are notoriously biased in our own favor. Because of that, we will never come to an experience of inner cleanness and full restoration until we come to the place of complete honesty before God. It was only after David had abjectly cried, "I have sinned!" that he gained absolution.

PLEA FOR RESTORATION—51:7-9

There are, in fact, a series of pleas.

"PURIFY ME WITH HYSSOP" (51:7)

Apparently the psalmist had in mind the ritual for the cleansing of the leper (Lev. 14:6-7). "As for the live bird, he shall take it, together with the cedar wood and the scarlet string and the hyssop, and shall dip them and the live bird in the blood of the bird that was slain over the running water. He shall then sprinkle seven times the one who is to be cleansed from the leprosy, and shall pronounce him clean."

David here appropriates such a cleansing for himself: "Wash me, and I shall be whiter than snow." Eyes, mind, imagination, will, and conscience all needed the cleansing of the blood. Nothing less than complete cleansing would satisfy him and relieve his guilty conscience.

"MAKE ME TO HEAR JOY AND GLADNESS" (51:8)

Coming from the lips of an adulterer and murderer, is the request not intolerable presumption? What right had he to be joyful and glad? But David knew that his was a God who delights in those who hope in His mercy. Such was his confidence that he asked for even more. "Let the bones which Thou hast broken rejoice" (lit., *dance*).

"HIDE THY FACE FROM MY SINS, AND BLOT OUT ALL MY INIQUITIES" (51:9)

For twelve dreary months he had willfully suffered the hiding of God's face; now David pleaded with God to turn toward him the light of His countenance and to hide His face from his sins. David wanted his stained record expunged, his pollution cleansed, his revolting disease healed.

PLEA FOR RENEWAL—51:10-12

David's heartbreaking experience produced a devastating sense of his inability to deal with the corruption of his heart, for there is no psychological manipulation that can make an unclean heart clean or remove the haunting sense of guilt and defilement that sin inevitably generates.

In his distress at the havoc his sin had brought in its wake and the sorrow he had caused to the heart of God, David saw clearly that nothing less than the supernatural intervention of God would meet his case. So he called in the Creator! Only the One who made the heart could meet the heart's need.

"CREATE IN ME A CLEAN HEART" (51:10)

He did not pray for a heart from which the principle of evil was completely eradicated. A pure heart is one in which no known, conscious, unjudged sin is tolerated and entertained. That experience is possible for us, too, but only on the grounds of Calvary's sacrifice and through the ministry of the Holy Spirit.

"RENEW A STEADFAST SPIRIT WITHIN ME" (51:10)

The implication is that he had experienced this blessing before but had forfeited it through his sin. "It was there before, Lord," he cries. "Put it there again!" A steadfast spirit is the fruit of which a pure heart is the root. David longed for a return to the old stability.

His prayer for his inner life also included a craving for *a willing spirit* (51:12)—a liberated spirit, freed from crippling inhibitions, a heart that embraced and enjoyed the will of God. He desired the blessing of *a broken spirit* (51:11). Not that he wished to become broken-spirited and dejected, but he did desire self-will to be crushed, the will of God to be dominant, all pride and arrogance exorcised and replaced by genuine humility.

"DO NOT CAST ME AWAY FROM THY PRESENCE" (51:11)

The misery of hell is the absence of God, as the joy of heaven is the presence of God. Love can endure anything but distance. Once the joy of intimacy with God has been experienced, life becomes unbearable without it. Now that he had regained divine favor, David could not bear the thought of losing it again. "Don't throw me away as a useless vessel," he entreated.

> Make use of me, my God
> Let me not be forgot,

> A broken vessel cast aside,
> One whom Thou usest not.
>
> Horatius Bonar

"DO NOT TAKE THY HOLY SPIRIT FROM ME" (51:11)

Christ's promise to his disciples was: "I will ask the Father, and He will give you another Helper, *that He may be with you forever*" (John 14:16, italics added). Since the descent of the Spirit on the day of Pentecost, no believing soul need fear that the Holy Spirit will be taken from him. He has come to abide with us forever. But God's people who lived under the Old Covenant enjoyed no such assurance, hence David's petition. He feared that He might be deprived of the Spirit's gracious ministry.

"RESTORE TO ME THE JOY OF THY SALVATION" (51:12)

We do not lose our salvation when we are betrayed into sin, but we do forfeit the joy that flows from uninhibited fellowship and intimacy with God. Once all is made right with God and man, the broken relationship is mended and the lost joy will once again flood the heart.

THE JOY OF RECOMMISSIONING—51:13-19

David had in faith appropriated the divine provision for restoration and renewal. His recaptured joy could not be contained; it had to find an outlet. He had to share his experience of salvation with others. Silence was unthinkable. "Then I will teach transgressors Thy ways" (v. 13). He was once again qualified to be a bearer of good news.

What a testimony he could now bear to the pardoning grace of God! To men who had failed grievously, he could say, "Take heart! See what my God had done for me. He will do no less for you." In that way, he was able to turn his trouble into treasure, and his sorrow into song.

> Who is a pardoning God like Thee?

> Or who has grace so rich and free?
>
> Samuel Davies

PASTOR TO BACKSLIDERS

And is that not the gracious way in which our loving Father still treats the truly penitent soul? After his failure, Peter was engulfed in self-reproach. So far as his witness was concerned, he could see no alternative to the scrapheap. But that was not his Master's view. "Simon, Simon, behold, Satan has demanded permission to sift you like wheat; but I have prayed for you, that your faith may not fail; and you, when once you have turned again, strengthen your brothers" (Luke 22:31-32).

In that single statement, Jesus assured Peter of His prayerful support, warned him of his temporary defection, and envisaged his subsequent recommissioning. The backslider was to become the pastor to backsliders. So, too, David, as a result of his experience of God's grace, would be able to strengthen his brethren, and sinners would be turned back to God (Psalm 51:13).

However, like Paul, David could not lightly shrug off his sense of blood-guiltiness. Paul mourned: "Not only did I lock up many of the saints in prisons, . . but also when they were being put to death, I cast my vote against them" (Acts 26:10). David cried: "Deliver me from bloodguiltiness, O God" (Psalm 51:14). If only he could be released from that haunting sense of guilt, nothing would deter him from proclaiming God's pardoning love to the penitent. "Then my tongue will joyfully sing of Thy righteousness."

The sense of pardon and release that God granted resulted in a grander conception of a God who has no delight in the mere observance of ritual (v. 16), but whose sole requirement is "a broken and a contrite heart" (v. 17). The important thing is not the meticulous observance of an external ritual, but the state of the offerer's heart. That is the sacrifice in which God finds delight, and that renders continuing intimacy with Him possible.

A humble, contrite, lowly heart,
  Believing, true and clean,
Which neither death nor life can part
  From Him who dwells within.

Charles Wesley

Notes

1. F. B. Meyer, *David* (London: Morgan & Scott, 1927), p. 171.

In the process of bringing salvation to the hearts of men, God is ever first. By His Spirit He invades the heart of the sinner. Thus the sinner who has now become a saint has received the power to abide in Christ. The words, "abide in Me" do not constitute a condition which man must fulfil in His own power before Christ will do His part. Far from it. It is sovereign grace from start to finish, but the responsibility of abiding in Christ is placed squarely upon man's shoulders, exactly where it belongs.[1]

William Hendriksen

7

Intimacy Is Maintained by Abiding

John 15

In the sacred discourse in the upper room, when Jesus bared His heart to His disciples, He stressed the necessity and possibility of maintaining the closest, most intimate fellowship with Himself. To illustrate, He told the parable of the vine and the branches, with its central lesson that only as the branch remained in the vine in intimate and vital contact, would it be fruitful.

> As the branch cannot bear fruit of itself, unless it abides in the vine, so neither can you, unless you abide in Me. [John 15:4]

A study of John 15 will reveal many important lessons relating to the theme of our study.

Abiding in Christ is, of course, possible only to real Christians. It means keeping unbroken contact with Christ in a union of intimate love. The word "abide" means simply "to remain, to stay, to continue, to cling to." It is as though the Lord was saying, "When you believed in Me, you were united to Me. Don't allow anything to break that intimate union. Keep constantly depending on Me." If the channel of union between vine and branch is blocked or broken, fruitfulness becomes impossible.

Note what our Lord stressed first in this significant passage.

OUR DUTY TO OURSELVES—15:1-11

THE TRUE VINE (v. 1)

"I am the true vine"—the real, the genuine vine, He claimed. Formerly, the nation of Israel had been referred to as a vine (Isa. 5:1-2). They had been planted "the choicest vine," but it had become degenerate and bore only worthless fruit, despite all the care and attention God had bestowed on it. The choice vine had become the worthless barren vine. "He expected it to produce good grapes, but it produced only worthless ones" (Isa. 5:2).

In contrast to the degenerate vine, Jesus claimed, "I am the genuine Vine," and then stated the essential condition of fruitfulness: "Abide in Me." The reason for that condition is that the vine can bear fruit only through the branches. To the amazed disciples, He made the breath-taking revelation: "I am the vine, *you are the branches*" (John 15:5, italics added)—united to the vine in intimate contact, sharing the same lifegiving sap.

THE UNFRUITFUL BRANCH (15:2-3)

"Every branch in Me that does not bear fruit, He takes away." The function of the vine is solely to bear fruit. "The vine lives to give its lifeblood." Its wood is useless for anything but fruit-bearing. If the branch fails there, it has no alternative function. It is cut off and burned.

In this paragraph, our Lord did not have salvation in view. His theme was fruitfulness. These verses do not teach that the unfruitful Christian will forfeit his salvation, but that he will lose his reward if his is a wasted life. Such branches are "cast . . . into the fire, and . . . burned" (15:6). Note that is not God but men who gather the unfruitful branches and burn them. The unfruitful Christian loses his influence for

God and his testimony to men. Hence the necessity of abiding in Christ.

THE FRUITFUL BRANCH (15:4-6)

To be fruitful, we must "abide in the Vine"—in vital union with the true vine, allowing nothing to come between us and Him. "Apart from Me," said Jesus, "you can do nothing" (v. 5). The absoluteness and finality of the statement is staggering. Not "very little," but "*nothing.*" Cut off from the source of the life-giving sap, we wither and die. Fruit is impossible when contact is broken.

Such a categorical statement should cause us to stop and ask ourselves whether we really are abiding and bearing fruit, or whether we are heading for the rubbish heap.

For a maximum yield, the branches of the vine need heavy pruning—heavier than most other trees. Unless it is severely cut back, the fruit will be sparse and poor. So God prunes the lives of His children, cuts back the rank growth of the self-life, not because He delights to see them suffer, but that their lives might be increasingly fruitful. He desires to see His children growing in spiritual maturity. There is to be a progression—"fruit, more fruit, much fruit."

> It is the branch that bears the fruit
>   That feels the knife,
> To prune it for a larger growth
>   And fuller life.*

Annie Johnson Flint

THE ABIDING IS TO BE RECIPROCAL (15:7)

"Abide in Me, and I in you" (15:4). "If you abide in Me, and My words abide in you. . ." (v. 7). This is a conditional promise of answered prayer: "Ask whatever you wish, and it shall be done for you." Christ in me—I in Christ—Christ's word abiding in me. That is intimacy indeed. With His Word constantly meditated on, loved, believed, and obeyed, we

---

*Used by permission of Evangelical Publishers, Toronto, Canada.

will increasingly receive and reflect the mind of Christ. His will will become ours, and our desires will be only what He desires.

The little daughter of a friend of the author one day said to her father, "Daddy, I do like to do what I do like to do!" That mutual and reciprocal abiding will mean that we will like to do what *He* likes us to do.

ABUNDANT FRUIT IS THE PROOF OF DISCIPLESHIP (15:8)

"By this My Father glorified that you bear much fruit, and so prove to be My disciples" (v. 8). Not all believers are true disciples, according to that statement. Our discipleship will be evidenced by our abiding in His love, enjoying it, reveling in it—a love as great as the Father has for the Son (15:10). Simple obedience is a secret of abiding in His love. Mutuality of love will inevitably result in a deepening intimacy.

ABOUNDING JOY RESULTS FROM ABIDING (15:11)

"I have spoken to you . . . that your joy may be made full," in other words, "that you may share with Me the joy I possess." Our joy is inextricably linked with His.

OUR DUTY TO EACH OTHER—15:12-17

WE ARE TO LOVE AS WE ARE LOVED (15:12)

"This is My commandment, that you love one another, just as I have loved you" (v. 12). But can love be thus commanded? Is it not spontaneous? Apparently love can be commanded, for our Lord did so. The answer to the problem lies in the fact that love does not spring from the emotions alone but also from the will. Erotic and romantic love may be mainly of the emotions, but the *agape* love spoken of here is on a higher level and deeply involves the will. Love for the unlovely and undeserving is not spontaneous, it springs from the will to love, *in spite of* the unloveliness.

An examination of the great love text, John 3:16, will support that contention. What prompted God's love for the world? Was it a happy, pleasurable emotion? Did He feel a warm glow in His heart at the thought of sending His Son to the death of the cross? Indeed, no. By a supreme act of His will, He chose to pluck out His heart, to sacrifice His only irreplaceable possession, His only Son, in order that we might be brought into intimate relationship with Him. That is the kind of love He expects us to show to one another. Christians should be characterized by fervent, mutual love. Not sloppy sentiment, but sacrificial love that expresses itself in loving activity to the unlovable as well as to the attractive.

The supreme test of love is not in overwhelming emotion, but willingness to lay down one's life for a friend. "Greater love has no one than this, that one lay down his life for his friends" (v. 13). Jesus was on the way to do just this—not for friends only, but also for enemies. Such love is not optional but obligatory. "We ought to lay down our lives for the brethren" (1 John 3:16).

Because love is commanded, it is possible, and Paul shares the enabling secret: "The love of God has been poured out within our hearts through the Holy Spirit who was given to us" (Rom. 5:5). Supernatural love is for us to appropriate and manifest to our fellows.

WE ARE CHRIST'S FRIENDS, NOT SERVANTS (15:14-15)

Here again we see the intimacy that comes from abiding. "No longer do I call you slaves . . . but I have called you friends." It is a friendship based on loving obedience.

Friends are friends because they share common tastes, ideals, and objectives. They share secrets with perfect confidence. Slaves do not share secrets with their masters, but friends do with their friends. Their relationship is relaxed and without inhibition. They find each other's company congenial. What a breathtaking conception of our relationship with our Lord! Those men who in a few hours were all to forsake Him and flee, He calls His friends. Amazing grace.

WE ARE CHOSEN, NOT CHOOSING (15:16)

"You did not choose Me, but I chose you." Our favored position is in no sense a reward for merit. It is the sovereign choice of our Master. Friends choose each other; their choice is mutual. But our Lord's choice of us was unilateral. He chose His disciples in the full knowledge of the instability and weakness they would display. It was no impulsive choice, for He made His selection after a night of prayer. He knew that the whole success of His program would depend upon the loyalty of those men. In coming testing days, the fact that they had been chosen by Him would prove a sheet anchor to them.

He also indicated that they were "chosen to bear fruit." It would be a lifework, and their effectiveness would depend on their prayer life. Prayer is still the open secret of "fruit that will last."

OUR DUTY TO SOCIETY—15:18-23

Our Lord here contrasts the fervent love of the disciple with the cold hatred and hostility of the world. "If the world hates you, you know that it has hated Me before it hated you," He counseled them.

THE WORLD AND THE CHURCH (15:18-19)

A Christian should not expect sympathy and consideration from a hostile, satanically-controlled society. Because a believer is identified with Christ, he should expect to share some of the hostility He experienced.

The world loves its own people, who adopt its standards and share its interests, but it hates those who will not conform (15:19). The early Christians who remained loyal to the faith were denounced as cannibals, immoral, disloyal revolutionaries, and incendiaries. Only when he compromises his position can a Christian maintain friendly relations with the world. Intimacy with Christ inevitably draws the hatred of the world, as His disciples discovered.

"A SLAVE IS NOT GREATER THAN HIS MASTER" (15:20-21)

Logically, the enemy of the master will be the enemy of his servant. He need not expect more considerate treatment than his master. The comforting factor is that our Master shares our rejection by the world, and appreciates the fact that it is because of our loyalty to Him. Nor will our loyalty lack its reward.

THE REASON FOR THE HATRED (15:22-23)

In a few terse words, Jesus diagnosed the cause of the world's hatred. If He had not come, they could have gone along comfortably in their sin, "but now they have no excuse for their sin." He had laid bare their hypocrisy, deceit, and malice and exposed their evil designs. Now they hated the Exposer and included His followers in their hostility. The world has never changed its attitude to both Master and servants. His witness to His Father (15:24) only served to deepen their causeless hatred.

How were the disciples to meet and overcome that hatred? Through the ministry of the Holy Spirit. "When the Helper comes, whom I will send to you from the Father . . . He will bear witness of Me, and you will bear witness also" (15:26-27). Jesus did not remove His disciples from this hostile world but empowered them for witness to it through the power of the Spirit (Acts 1:8). That power is equally available for those disciples who are the objects of the world's hostility in this day.

Notes

1. William Hendriksen, *Gospel of John* (London: Banner of Truth, 1954), p. 299.

"It pleased God to reveal His Son in me." The apostle knew too much of the divine life to admit that the vast change in him could be entirely accounted for by what he had seen with his mortal, and now blinded eyes. He was aware that a true and lasting work can only be achieved when the inner eye has perceived things that are hidden from mortal sense. In other words, God, who commanded light to shine out of darkness must shine in the heart "to give the light of the knowledge of His glory in the face of Jesus." [1]

F. B. Meyer

8

Intimacy Is Fostered by the Holy Spirit

John 15:26; 16:13-14

It must have been a shattering experience for our Lord's disciples when He broke the news that He would shortly leave them. And His statements were so enigmatic! "I go to prepare a place for you." "Where I go, you cannot follow Me now; but you shall follow later." "You heard that I said to you, 'I go away, and I will come to you.' If you loved Me, you would have rejoiced, because I go to the Father" (John 14:2; 13:36; 14:28).

What could He mean? How could they be glad when the light of their life was going out? How could they face a menacing, hostile world without His supporting presence? Who else could fill the place He held in their affections? It must have seemed a strangely hollow assurance when He told them, "It is to your advantage that I go away" (John 16:7). But could anything be more in their interests than His continued presence with them? How could the loss of a mother be for the good of her children? Small wonder that the icy hand of despair clutched at the disciples' hearts as they contemplated their lost intimacy with Him.

No more to see Thy face—to meet no more,
Till on that undiscovered, unknown shore

To turn to life again, and toil our day,
Glory so distant still, and Thou away,
While earth's dark future on us frowns, all viewed
As one severe extended solitude.

                                        Anonymous

ANOTHER COUNSELOR

His promise of "another Counselor" afforded them some comfort, but they could not see how it could be fulfilled. "I will not leave you as orphans; I will come to you" (John 14:18), He had said. But what did that cryptic statement mean?

An orphan has known a father, mother, and the warmth of family love but has lost them. That was how the disciples would picture themselves if He were to leave them. Although they could not understand it, they clung to His promise that they would not be left orphans with no one to care for them.

"Now I am going to Him who sent Me," He told them. "If I do not go away, the Helper will not come to you; but if I go, I will send Him to you" (John 16:5, 7). Just as an orphaned child needs someone to comfort, support, and counsel him, so Jesus promised the Holy Spirit to be Counselor and Guide to his friends in their desolation and loss.

Further, He told them that in answer to His prayer on their behalf, the Father would give them "another Helper" (John 14:16), or *Paraclete*, as the word is in Greek. Not a *different* Counselor, but *another* Counselor. It means "another of the same kind." Jesus was one Paraclete (1 John 2:1), and the Holy Spirit was another of exactly the same kind—in fact, He was our Lord's other self. Thus, He indicated that the Holy Spirit was just like Himself.

J. I. Packer wrote:

> A *Comforter*—the richness of the idea is seen from the variety of renderings in different translations, "counsellor" (RSV)

"helper" (Moffatt) "advocate" (Weymouth), one "to befriend you" (Knox). The thoughts of encouragement, support, assistance, care, and the shouldering of responsibility for another's welfare, are all conveyed by this word. *Another* Comforter—yes, because Jesus was their original Comforter, and the newcomer's task was to continue this side of His ministry . . . He will care for you, Christ was saying in effect, in the way that I have cared for you.[2]

That loving provision was made by the Lord, not only to console them in their sense of loss, but to make possible a continuance of the intimacy with Him that they had enjoyed. When on earth, He was geographically limited. He could not be in two places at the same time. While He was having a private interview with Peter, the other disciples were denied His fellowship. Then, too, His influence on them could be only *external*. But when the other Counselor came, they would exchange His physical presence for His omnipresence. The Holy Spirit knows no physical limitations but is equally available to all God's people, wherever they are and whatever their need.

Our Lord's departure from earth made possible a deeper, more constant intimacy with Him, even than what they had experienced when He was with them.

A CHRISTOCENTRIC MINISTRY

The ministry of the Spirit is essentially Christocentric. His primary concern is to glorify Christ and to secure the acknowledgment and practical manifestation of His lordship in our lives. Although He cannot add anything to the glories of the exalted Christ, He can make Him real and glorify Him in the experience of His followers. It is one of His functions to reveal and explain Him.

"What light is to the earth, the Holy Spirit is to Christ," said Joseph Parker. One cannot see a person in a dark room. But let someone switch on the light and the person stands revealed. The Spirit delights to illumine the face of Jesus Christ as He is revealed in the Scriptures He has inspired.

No Rivalry in the Godhead

There is no rivalry within the unity of the Godhead. Scripture represents each of the three divine Persons as delighting to honor the other. Christ's passion was to manifest the hidden excellence of the Father. "I do not seek My glory," He claimed. "If I glorify Myself, My glory is nothing" (John 8:50, 54). His work on earth reached its zenith when He prayed to His Father, "I glorified Thee on the earth, having accomplished the work which Thou hast given Me to do" (John 17:4).

Jesus prayed, "Father, the hour has come; glorify Thy Son. . . . And now, glorify Thou Me together with Thyself, Father" (John 17:1, 5). In answering the caviling Jews, He told them, "It is My Father who glorifies Me, of whom you say, 'He is our God' " (John 8:54). Thus the Father glorifies the Son.

The Spirit glorifies the Son, even as the Son glorified the Spirit by saying that He would come as His own personal Representative. "He shall glorify Me; for He shall take of Mine, and shall disclose it to you" (16:14). "When the Helper comes, whom I will send to you from the Father, that is the Spirit of truth, who proceeds from the Father, He will bear witness of Me" (15:26).

Thus with a blessed mutuality the members of the Godhead accord honor and glory to each other. As the supreme Lover of Christ, the Holy Spirit is jealous of His glory and interests. He cannot bear to see a waning or cooling love for the Lord, and so, as we give Him opportunity, He fans the fire of our devotion.

How does the Holy Spirit show us the things of Christ and make Him real to us? It is preeminently in the Scriptures that He reveals the things of Christ. To the Spirit-anointed eye of the diligent student of the Word, the Old Testament is seen to be full of Christ, every page revealing some new facet of His person and work. In the prophets, His greatness and achievements, as well as His sufferings and glory, were anticipated. Through meditating on the Word, a Spirit-taught believer can again experience the burning heart kindled in the hearts of the Emmaus disciples, when Jesus, "beginning with Moses and with all the prophets . . . explained to them the things concerning Himself in all the Scriptures" (Luke 24:27). Under the illumination of the inspiring Spirit, the words become spirit and life.

Dr. A. B. Simpson clarified the Spirit's function.

> The great business of the Holy Spirit is to stand behind the scenes and make Jesus real. Just as the telescope reveals not itself, but the stars beyond, so Christ is revealed by the Holy Spirit, as the medium of our spiritual vision. . . . Through the telephone of prayer, we may catch the very voice of our absent Master and be conscious of the heart-throbs of His love. . . . The presence of the Comforter but makes Him nearer and dearer, and enables us to realize and know that we are in Him and He in us.[3]

THE INTERIOR REVELATION

The Spirit is not content with a mere exterior or external revelation of Christ to the believing heart. On the Damascus road, Christ was revealed *to* Paul, to the accompaniment of "a light from heaven, brighter than the sun," blazing around him and his companions (Acts 26:13). He saw with his physical eyes the ascended Christ and with his ears heard Him speak. It was no hallucination, the product of a heated imagination. But external vision was not sufficient. His transforming experience, cataclysmic though it was, turning implacable hatred to adoring worship, must be applied to his heart.[4] And that is what happened.

Writing of his experience he said, "But when [God] who had set me apart, even from my mother's womb, and called me through His grace, was pleased *to reveal His Son in me,* that I might preach Him among the Gentiles. . ." (Gal. 1:15, 16, italics added). The words "To reveal His Son *in me*" mean vastly more than "to my intellect." The phrase has reference to *illumining* grace ("to reveal") which is at the same time *transforming*.

The result of that interior revelation of Christ meant for Paul a deepened sense of the presence of Christ, "intimately, ravishingly near."

Paul had already seen Christ exalted at the hand of God, but now He was revealed to Him by the Holy Spirit as dwelling in his unworthy heart. From that moment, there was a new dimension in his experience. "It is no longer I who live, but Christ lives in me" (Gal. 2:20). In this glorious fact lay, in large measure, the explanation of his flaming ministry.

There is always a moral basis for such a revelation.

> It is to the man who loves Him that Jesus reveals Himself even more fully. Obedient, trusting love leads to a fuller and a fuller revelation. . . . No evil man can receive the revelation of God. He can be used by God, but he can have no fellowship with God. It is only to the man who is looking for Him that God reveals Himself. . . . Fellowship with God, the revelation of God are dependent on love; and love is dependent on obedience. [5]

But the Holy Spirit does not rest content with a mere *revelation of Christ*. His objective is a *reproduction of Christ* in the life of the believer. With this in view, He patiently works until Christ is formed in each (4:19).

When an egg is laid, amid the fluid there floats a tiny speck of life. As the egg is incubated, the embryo gradually develops, while the fluid diminishes. At the end of three weeks, no trace of fluid is left. The fully-formed chick pecks its way out of the confining shell and embarks on life in a new world.

When the new life enters the believing heart, it is an embryo life that must be nurtured on the "pure milk of the Word" (1 Pet. 2:2). Through devout meditation on Scripture and seasons of waiting on God, the Holy Spirit fosters and develops that life from within, until the likeness of Christ is more and more apparent without.

> Spirit of Jesus, glorify,
>> The Master's name in me;
> Whether I live or if I die,
>> Let Christ exalted be.

> Author Unknown

Notes

1. F. B. Meyer, *Paul* (London: Morgan & Scott, 1910), p. 57.
2. J. I. Packer, *Knowing God* (London: Hodder & Stoughton, 1973), p. 68.
3. A. B. Simpson, *The Holy Spirit* (Harrisburg: Christian Publications, 1924), 2:62.
4. William Hendriksen, *Galatians* (Grand Rapids: Baker, 1968), p. 52.
5. William Barclay, *The Gospel of John* (Edinburgh: St. Andrew, 1955), p. 197.

The Galatians were living with reference to the Spirit in the sense that the new divine life resident in their beings, was supplied by the Spirit. Now, Paul says, "In view of the fact that you have a new life principle operating in your beings, then walk by the Spirit."

Thus the exhortation is to the Galatians . . . to conduct themselves under the guidance, impulses and energy of the new life. Here we have the free will of the Christian and his responsibility to live the highest type of Christian life, and the grace of God which will make that possible.[1]

Kenneth S. Wuest

9

Intimacy Involves Walking in the Spirit

Galatians 5:16, 25

The Holy Spirit plays a crucial role in sanctifying and maintaining us in fellowship with God. Scripture clearly teaches that our enjoyment of full salvation is dependent on our "walking in the Spirit."

It is one thing to step out into the Christian life, but quite another to maintain a consistent, intimate walk with God. The step must lengthen out into a walk, and that cannot be learned in ten easy lessons.

WALKING IN THE SPIRIT

But I say, walk by the Spirit, and you will not carry out the desire of the flesh. For the flesh sets its desire against the Spirit, and the Spirit against the flesh; for these are in opposition to one another, so that you may not do the things that you please. [Gal. 5:16-17]

In Galatians 5, walking in the Spirit is set in apposition to walking after the desires of the flesh. "Walk" is a familiar Bible term for daily living. When the record says that Enoch walked with God, it means that he lived his daily life in unbroken fellowship with God.

In Galatians 5:16, the ordinary word for "walking around" is used. It stands for a person's conduct in ordinary life, his daily actions at home or in business, at work or play, and walking denotes activity and progress.

The implication is that in our daily life we are to live in constant awareness of the presence of the Holy Spirit. It is as if Paul were saying, "Habitually order your life-style through the Spirit's guidance, and then you will not be deflected by the desires of the flesh, from a walk in fellowship with God."

A clear example of the outworking of such walking in the Spirit is seen in Acts 16:6-10. Paul, Silas, and Timothy were on a missionary tour and had planned to visit the west coast of Asia Minor, but they were "forbidden by the Holy Spirit to speak the Word in Asia." Next, "They were trying to go into Bithynia, and the Spirit of Jesus did not permit them; and passing by Mysia, they came down to Troas." There they conferred together and sought the Spirit's alternative direction. They had received negative guidance, but now they wanted positive direction, and they received it.

Paul was given a vision of a man calling, "Come over to Macedonia and help us." After Paul had seen the vision, "immediately we sought to go into Macedonia, concluding that God had called us to preach the gospel to them."

The apostolic team was sensitive to the voice of the Spirit. We are not told exactly how the Holy Spirit conveyed His directions and prohibitions to them, but the Spirit-filled person will recognize and obey the Spirit's voice.

The Greek word for "walk" in Galatians 5:25 signifies more than mere motion. "Since we live by the Spirit, let us keep in step with the Spirit" (NIV). It signifies a measured walk, marching in file or in step. The idea is that of *concerted action* or joint effort. "Let us keep in step with the Spirit." When we set out together with our fellow believers, we are to let the Holy Spirit be the One who gives the orders. And we are to keep in step with each other. The tense of the verb implies: "Let us go on walking by the Spirit"—habitually walking along the line drawn by the Spirit. We are thus to walk in obedience to His leading and in dependence on His power.

When combined, the words from verses 16 and 25 would mean that we are to recognize the Holy Spirit as the guide of our personal lives in all our decisions and actions. When we engage in concerted action with others, as in the above case of the apostolic team, it is the Holy Spirit who is to order and discipline our combined effort. Walking in and by the Spirit involves implicit obedience to His promptings.

When we make mistakes in our personal lives, or when relationships with others in a joint effort break down, the implication is either that we have not sought or have not obeyed the Spirit's leading.

THE ANTAGONISM OF FLESH AND SPIRIT

> The flesh sets its desires against the Spirit, and the Spirit against the flesh; for these are in opposition to one another. [Gal. 5:17]

What is meant by "the flesh"? Dr. W. G. Scroggie detected ten shades of meaning used in the Bible. In nine of the ten, there is no ethical or theological content. But the tenth, which is the one Paul mainly employs, does have such significance. The flesh may be defined as "man's fallen nature as under the power of sin." It is the evil principle in man's nature, the traitor within who is in league with the attackers without. The flesh provides the tinder on which the devil's temptations can kindle.

In man there are two conflicting principles, each of which strives for the mastery. It is impossible for them to live together in peaceful coexistence. One principle is carnal; the other is spiritual. One is the principle of fleshly energy. The other is the principle of complete domination by the Holy Spirit. Our wills have the responsibility of choosing whether the carnal or the spiritual shall have the ascendancy.

The only remedy for the fleshly, or carnal, nature is that it be crucified, for it is inveterately wicked and incapable of improvement. But how can that be done, for crucifixion is a death that cannot be self-inflicted? That is true also in the spiritual realm. But it has been achieved in the death of Christ.

"We *have been* with Him through baptism. . . . We *have become united* with Him in the likeness of His death. . . . Knowing this, that our old self was crucified with him . . . that we should no longer be slaves to sin" (Rom. 6:4-6, italics added). It is not left to us to crucify the flesh or self-life; that was done for us in Christ's death, But it remains for us to reckon it to be true for us (6:11). As we take that ground in faith, the Holy Spirit will make it true in experience, and we shall be emancipated from the dominance of fleshly desires.

WORKS OF THE FLESH OR FRUIT OF THE SPIRIT?

When we walk "after the flesh," we will inexorably produce the works of the flesh (Gal. 5:19-21). Paul divided those works into five sordid categories:

Gross physical sins:	sexual immorality, impurity, and debauchery
Occult practices:	idolatry, witchcraft
Evil dispositions:	hatred, discord, jealousy, fits of rage
Religious disunity:	selfish ambition, dissensions, factions, and envy
Sensual indulgence:	drunkenness, orgies, and the like.

It is sobering to reflect that any of those sins is possible to a believer who is not walking in the Spirit. Quite probably some of them would have been actual but for the Spirit's restraint.

When, however, we walk in the Spirit, He is no longer

hampered by our carnality and disobedience and is able to produce the fruit of the Spirit in us in increasing abundance (Gal. 5:22-23). Paul divided those fruits into three triads.

With reference to
experience: love, joy, and peace
With reference to *conduct*:   patience, kindness, goodness
With reference to *character*: faithfulness, gentleness, and
                                self-control.

The presence of those qualities in our lives makes possible increasing intimacy with God in whom all are present in infinite perfection.

It is worthy of note that "the Spirit" occurs seven times in Galatians 5:16-25, and in each case it is not the human spirit but the Holy Spirit who is in view. The Spirit is always the friend, as the flesh is the foe, of true holiness. As we walk in the Spirit, we acquire new tastes and desires that fit us for fellowship with God.

VICTORY OVER THE FLESH

Walking in the Spirit does not mean that we will be immune from the pull of fleshy desires. When the Spirit fills us, He does take control of our personality, but He does not dehumanize us. The desires will assert themselves, but we will be enabled by the Spirit's strengthening to refrain from gratifying them. We are still in the field of battle, but we no longer fight alone. We have a powerful though unseen Ally on whom to rely.

A walk in the Spirit will of necessity be *a walk in accordance with the Word* the Spirit has inspired. The parallel between Ephesians 5:18-21 and Colossians 3:16-17 is significant. The same results are said to flow from being filled with the Spirit in the first case, and being filled with the Word in the second. To remain filled with the Spirit, and thus enjoy His continuing sanctifying work, will mean continuing to be filled with the Word. The relationship is obvious.

It will also be *a walk in obedience to the divine will*. That is basic. The Lord will not admit to His intimate fellowship those who walk in disobedience, for that grieves the Spirit and forfeits His aid.

As we walk by the Spirit, following His promptings, the voice of fleshly desire will lose its power to allure. In his book *White Fang*, Jack London told of an animal of that name who was half-wolf, half-dog. One day White Fang strayed into a hen-run and killed several hens. The owner was naturally very angry. White Fang's trainer said to him, "I will guarantee that he will remain a whole afternoon in the hen-run and not kill a single chicken."

The test began. Whenever the old lust to kill asserted itself, his master's voice recalled White Fang again and again, until at last the force of the impulse had spent itself as he listened to that quietly restraining voice. He finally fell asleep in the midst of the hens. When he woke up, he yawned and jumped out of the hen-run. The temptation had no more power to allure. White Fang's victory over his wolf-nature sprang from the restraining power of his loved master's voice. So with us. Sensitive obedience to the restraining and empowering voice of the Spirit brings victory.

That is not the mere damming back of the temptation, only for it to break out once again, worse than ever. It is the counteracting operation of a higher and more powerful law (Rom. 8:2).

That principle was powerfully illustrated in the Greek myths of Ulysses and the sirens, and Jason and the Argonauts.

When Ulysses and his men set out on their journey of conquest, they were warned by Circe to avoid the sirens at all costs. She told them that the sirens' voices were alluring but fatal to all who stopped to listen. The unfortunate listeners became rooted like a tree and could not tear themselves away, until they died of hunger.

"Fill your companions' ears with wax," she counseled. "If you yourself want to listen to their song, first let your men bind you securely to the mast." Ulysses heeded her advice. "If the melody beguiles me," he ordered them, "I charge you, disobey my word, and bend more strongly to your oars."

At length Ulysses heard the beautiful strains that stole into his mind, overpowered his body, and overcame his will. As the music came sweeter and sweeter, Ulysses' love for home weakened. He struggled with his shame, but at last the bewitching voices of the sirens prevailed.

"Loose me and let me stay with the sirens!" he raged. He threatened and entreated; he promised his men mountains of gold with desperate signs and gestures. His men only bound him more securely. He raged and tore at his bonds, for it was agony for him to leave the spot. But not until the last sound of music died away did they loose him. He had passed out of the zone of temptation.

Jason with his Argonauts set out in search of the Golden Fleece. Medea warned Jason and his men of the menace of the sirens, as they began to hear their bewitching strains. All around they could see the shore strewn with the bones of those who had succumbed to the sirens' charms.

On board the boat was Orpheus, the king of minstrels. "Let them match their songs with mine," he challenged the three maidens whom they could see, and whose silvery voices stole over the moonlit waters.

There were seagulls in long lines and shoals of fish that came to listen. The oars of Jason's heroes fell from their hypnotized hands. Their heads drooped, and their heavy eyes closed.

Then Medea cried to Orpheus, "Sing louder! Wake up these sluggards!" Orpheus struck his skillful hand over the strings of his lyre, and his voice rose like a trumpet. The music penetrated the souls of the infatuated men, and their souls thrilled. Orpheus kept on singing until his voice completely drowned the voices of the sirens. Once again the Argonauts took up their oars, and Jason and his men sailed to victory.

"Sing the song again, Orpheus," they cried. "We will dare and suffer to the last."

Those stories strikingly illustrate two possible ways of gaining victory over the desires of the flesh. One is the way of *negations and prohibitions*. They are of some help and have their place. Ulysses was bound, otherwise he would have yielded to the cravings of his heart. His men had wax in their ears, or they too would have yielded. The teachings of Buddha and Confucius could bring us as far as that. But it is an incontrovertible fact that to concentrate the mind on the desires of the flesh, if only to conquer them, seems to intensify the desires.

How much better is the Orphean music than the Ulyssian wax! With the heavenly Orpheus on board, as we listen to His heavenly music, the voices of the sirens lose the power of their appeal, and our spirits are free.

It is all a matter of who is in control of the life. The self-life with its unlawful desires and tendencies is the citadel of the fleshly principle, and it will continue to dominate until it is consigned to the cross. In the very passage we have been studying, Paul wrote: "Those who belong to Christ Jesus have crucified the flesh with its passions and desires" (Gal. 5:24). That is involved in walking by the Spirit and results in our emancipation from yielding to the desires of the flesh.

Notes

1. Kenneth S. Wuest, *Galatians in the Greek New Testament* (Chicago: Moody, 1944), p. 162.

God is not satisfied until all His family love Him, and all His children love one another. No earthly father could really be content with less. If any of His children were cold towards him, or at feud with one another, then the parent's heart must be sad. [1]

Harrington C. Lees

10

Intimacy Demands Reciprocal Love

One Saturday evening the saintly Samuel Rutherford was conducting family devotions in his Scottish home when there was a knock on the door. The stranger was warmly welcomed and invited to join the family circle. Questions from the Scottish catechism were being asked and answered. When the visitor's turn came, his question was "How many commandments are there?"

"Eleven," he replied.

Rutherford was amazed that a man so evidently well-educated should be so ignorant, so he corrected him.

In reply the stranger said, "A new commandment I give to you, that love you love one another."

Rutherford was startled at the response.

Next morning as Rutherford walked along the path to the church, behind the hedge he heard a voice in supplication and recognized it as the voice of his visitor.

"Who are you?" Rutherford asked when the stranger emerged.

"My name is Ussher."

He was the primate of Ireland, to whom we largely owe our Bible chronology. In explaining his presence, the bishop said, "I had heard so much of your piety that I chose this way of judging for myself."

Their hearts flowed together in devotion to their common Lord. He invited the bishop to preach, and, not surprisingly, his text was John 13:34, "A new commandment I give to you, that you love one another."

THE NATURE OF LOVE

Mutual love is of the essence of intimacy. Where there is no love, there is no intimacy. Unfortunately, the word *love* as commonly used has become sadly debased and misunderstood. The romantic or erotic aspects of love are predominant in modern literature and in common parlance. In its essence, love is "the self-imparting quality in the nature of God that moves Him to seek the highest good of His creatures, in whom He seeks to awake responsive love." Because of that, love is basic to our knowledge of and intimacy with God. "The one who does not love does not know God, for God is love" (1 John 4:8). Love is grounded in the nature of God and is the highest expression of character. We are mature only to the degree that we are mature in love.

> Thy heart is opened wide,
> Its offered love most free,
> That heart to heart I may abide,
> And hide myself in Thee:
> Ah, how Thy love doth burn,
> Till I that love return,
> I would love Thee as Thou lovest me,
> O Jesus, most desired.

Love is more than sentiment; it is an activity. It must express itself, sacrifice itself, pour itself out on another. It is essentially unselfish and outgoing. God's love moved Him to sacrificial action. "This is how God showed His love among us: He sent His one and only Son into the world that we might live through Him" (1 John 4:9, NIV). His love impels and constrains Him to seek the lost and recover the wanderers.

Paganism does not produce selfless love. The Japanese language had no word to express Christian love; another word had to be coined. The Tasmanian natives, now extinct, had no word for love, but many different words for infanticide. Indeed, the New Testament word for love, *agape*, had to be filled with new content to express that essentially Christian grace.

THE ORIGIN OF LOVE

For fifty years, John had been musing on and contemplating the mystery of God's love for sinning men. To him, it was still incredible that a holy God should be willing to maintain intimate relations with sinful men. It still overwhelmed him. In mixed awe and ecstasy, he exclaimed: "See how great a love the Father has bestowed upon us" (1 John 3:1). The word John uses here signifies "of what country or race." God's love is exotic and is not indigenous to the barren, cold soil of our hearts. It comes from another, warmer climate. Only heaven could produce so fragrant a bloom. "Love is of God," he adds. The Christmas carol "Love Came Down at Christmas" expresses the truth that for the first time God's love was free to fully manifest itself in all its charm and winsomeness.

THE PRIMACY OF LOVE

Our Lord accorded love first place in the scale of ethical values. In referring to the two commandments to love God and our fellow men, Jesus said: "The foremost is. . . . There is no other commandment greater than these" (Mark 12:29, 31). Paul added his confirmation: "But now abide faith, hope, love, these three; but the greatest of these is love" (1 Cor. 13:13).

Because love is central in His own nature, it is not surprising that God requires it to be central in man. Scripture emphasizes that God loves us with all His heart, and He longs for us to love Him with all our powers and capacities—with heart, soul, mind, and strength.

THE HEART IS THE SEAT OF OUR EMOTIONAL NATURES

The degree in which our emotions are involved may vary with different temperaments, but there must be some degree of involvement.

F. W. Faber, the mystic, wrote these glowing lines:

> O Jesus, Jesus, dearest Lord,
> Forgive me if I say,
> For very love Thy sacred name
> A thousand times a day.
>
> Burn, burn O love within my heart
> Burn fiercely night and day
> Till all the dross of earthly love
> Is burned, and burned away.

Not everyone can rise to such heights of rapturous devotion. Not everyone experiences the passionate love of Samuel Rutherford. But although we may not attain such a level of love, our emotions must be engaged. We are to put not only intellect but emotion into our worship. A cold heart cannot truly worship.

THE SOUL IS THE SEAT OF OUR VOLITIONAL NATURES

Genuine love for God is more than a pleasing stirring of the emotions. It will involve the whole strength of our moral natures. God's love moved Him to exercise His will to make an infinitely costly sacrifice. The will must be engaged.

THE MIND IS THE SEAT OF OUR INTELLECTUAL NATURES

The flame of our love for God and our fellow men must be fed by fuel provided by the mind. Our love for and worship of God must not be merely intuitive. We must put intelligence into it. Paul says, "I shall pray with the spirit and I shall pray with the mind also" (1 Cor. 14:15).

THE STRENGTH OF OUR PHYSICAL NATURES WILL ALSO BE ENGAGED

We are to love and worship God with "all our being's ransomed powers." We are to put intensity and zeal into our worship.

It is evident that with varying temperaments, one or more

of those qualities may be more prominent than others. That fact has caused someone to say that one who loves with the emotions only will be a sentimentalist. One who loves with the will only will be legalistic. And one who loves with the intellect only will have little warmth. God desires the love of the whole personality.

With all thy heart, with all thy soule and mind,
Thou must Him love, and His behests embrace;
All other loves—with which the world doth blind
Weake fancies, and stirre up affections base—
Thou must renounce, and utterly displace;
And give thyself unto Him full and free,
That full and freely gave Himself to thee.

Edmund Spenser

THE PATTERN OF LOVE

Christ sets His own love before us as a model. "A new commandment I give to you, that you love one another, even as I have loved you, that you also love one another" (John 13:34). The law of love goes far further than loving one's neighbors as oneself; it is to love one another as Himself! It is love that takes no thought of the cost. That was the active principle of Christ's life. Paul, too, exhorts us to "live a life of love, just as Christ loved us and gave Himself up for us as a fragrant offering and sacrifice to God" (Eph. 5:2, NIV).

Affinities and aversions have nothing to do with love. We are to love people whom we do not even like! "If you love those who love you, what credit is that to you? For even sinners love those who love them" (Luke 6:32). Although I may not like a person, I can still will to love him. It is the will and not the emotions that is supreme.

THE TEST OF LOVE

"He who has My commandments and keeps them, he it is who loves Me, and he who loves Me shall be loved by My

Father, and I will love him, and will disclose Myself to him" (John 14:21). Obedience is the test of love, and it is rewarded by deepening intimacy. Nothing is said about emotional reactions—only simple obedience. The key question is not, "How do you feel?" but, "Have you obeyed?" Love is expressed through the will. If we are living obediently, we have John 14:21 as our assurance that we love Him and He loves us—even if we are unable to rise to the emotional heights of F. W. Faber's beautiful hymn.

One timid Christian said, "I think I love Him because there are things I refrain from doing for no other reason than that He forbids them, while I do other things simply because He desires them." He passes the test. If Christ's will is to us the law of our lives, His smile of approval will be an adequate reward.

The Impartation of Love

THE FATHER'S GIFT

"See how great a love the Father has bestowed upon us, that we should be called children of God" (1 John 3:1). It is love not merely exhibited but actually imparted to us. We are endowed with that incredible love.

IN ANSWER TO THE SON'S PRAYER

Human love is moonlike; it has no light of its own. It is derived from a divine Source. In His sacerdotal prayer Jesus said, "I have made Thy name known to them, and will make it known; that the love where with Thou didst love Me may be in them, and I in them" (John 17:26).

IMPARTED THROUGH THE SPIRIT'S MEDIATION

"The love of God has been poured out within our hearts through the Holy Spirit who was given to us" (Rom. 5:5). Our unaided love can never attain to the divine desire nor reach the depths of human need. But our union with Christ makes that possible. His love is being perpetually poured into our hearts by the Holy Spirit. It is for us to believe and act on that glorious fact, and it will become true not in theory only but in actual experience.

But here a problem arises. Some may question that, if that is true, why are we often so loveless, with little deep affection for God and concern for fellow men?

The fact is that our love is totally inadequate. The peculiarities of unlovely people, instead of kindling love in us, arouse our aversion. God's love alone is adequate, and that is what the Holy Spirit has infused into us.

Love is the fruit of the Spirit. That fruit is not the product of painful striving, but of simple abiding in Christ, as earlier noted. Indeed, each element in the fruit of the Spirit (Gal. 5:22-23) is but a different facet of love. Joy is love's song. Peace is love's repose. Patience is love's endurance. Kindness is love's sympathy. Goodness is love's self-forgetfulness. Faithfulness is love's trustworthiness. Self-control is love's discipline.

It is in the expression of *agape* love that healing of divisions may be found. On one occasion, the Moravian church in Germany was threatened with dissension. Count Zinzendorf suggested that instead of argument, they should meet together and study the first epistle of John. Day after day they met and read; then on August 13, 1727, a great thing happened.

They went to Berthelsdorf for their love feast, their *agape*. As they spoke and prayed, the place where they were assembled was shaken, and a thrill went through the waiting company. They turned to each other and said, "*What is this*? Surely this must be the Spirit of Pentecost." Afterward, when they were asked to describe what had happened, they answered, "That day we learned to love: to love Christ and to love each other." And they never yet have returned to their argument. Instead of disputing, they started a prayer meeting which, in relays, lasted without intermission for over a hundred years.

Notes

1. Harrington C. Lees, *The Practice of the Love of God* (London: Robert Scott, 1915), p. 11.

Delay, with its apparent destruction of all hope, can be a deep discipline to the soul that would serve the Lord Jesus. We live in a restless, impatient day. We have little time for preparation and less for worship. We feel we must be active, energetic, enthusiastic and humanly effective; and we cannot understand why inactivity, weariness, weakness and seeming uselessness should become our lot. It all appears to be so futile and foolish, without plan and purpose. . . .

Let the darkness of delay discipline your soul in the patience of the saints in the promises of God who will not suffer His promises to fail. [1]

V. R. Edman

11

Intimacy Is Deepened by Discipline

Hebrews 12:5-11

One of the Scriptures' mysterious and challenging statements is that of Hebrews 5:8-9: "Although He was a Son, He learned obedience from the things which He suffered; and having been made perfect, He became to all those who obey Him the source of eternal salvation." His sufferings were apparently the means of His perfecting. It will not be otherwise with His disciples.

"FOR THOSE WHOM THE LORD LOVES HE DISCIPLINES" (12:6).

Just as a caring parent will lovingly discipline and train his child, so God lovingly disciplines us. We live in a world of mystery and unexplained enigmas, so it is not surprising that the element of mystery should invade this realm too. Indeed, our Lord indicated that it would be so. "What I do you do not realize now; but you shall understand hereafter" (John 13:7). If we are to experience serenity in this turbulent world, we will need to take firmer grasp of God's sovereignty and trust His love even when we cannot discern His purpose. We must remember that the hand molding the clay is nail-pierced, and that our God's sovereignty will never clash with His paternity. "But now, O LORD, Thou art our Father, we are the clay, and Thou our potter" (Isa. 64:8). If we are to enjoy a deepening intimacy with God, we must react to His providential dealings in a spiritual way, even though they may be inscrutable. These dealings may take various forms, but all are planned in love, and with a view to cultivating a deeper intimacy with God. "[God] disciplines us for our good, that we may share His holiness" (Heb. 12:10).

THE DISCIPLINE OF DISTURBANCE

We live in a very security-conscious age, so we endeavor to protect and insure ourselves against any unwelcome contingencies. Our affluent society makes abundant provision for us to enjoy our leisure and pleasures. We love to settle down in our fur-lined ruts and enjoy our comforts, which are only mildly disturbed by the tragic world around us. A good home, late model car, pleasant recreations, happy holidays, congenial friends all tend to make heaven less attractive and the material to take the ascendancy over the spiritual.

But affluence and comfort often prove to be the foes of faith. Not that there is anything wrong with these things in themselves, for God "richly supplies us with all things to enjoy" (1 Tim. 6:17). But unless we are on our guard, they become the chief end of life, and God and His Kingdom are gradually relegated to a minor place. To counteract that dangerous tendency, our loving Father at times disturbs the even tenor of our way. He is concerned that we should not miss the best in life.

In the song of Moses that principle is illustrated. "Like an eagle that stirs up its nest, that hovers over its young, He spread His wings and caught them, He carried them on His pinions. The LORD alone guided him" (Deut. 32:11-12).

As with the eagle, so with the Lord. The eagle builds its nest on the mountain crag, using first sticks and twigs, then lining it carefully with fur, feathers, and grass. The little eaglets hatch out into an ideally comfortable home. Life is perfect. Meals are delivered regularly. There is nothing to be desired.

But one day the mother eagle appears to go berserk and tears away the soft lining of nest, leaving only sticks, twigs, and thorns. The fledglings are mystified at the change in their mother. The nest becomes so uncomfortable that they climb up to the edge of the nest and look down at the forbidding rocks below. Suddenly, the mother eagle gives one of them a push, and it goes tumbling through space to certain death. But swifter than the fall is the mother's flight. Just in time, she swoops down, catching the eaglet on her wings, and bears it up to safety on the mountain crag. As an eagle, so the Lord.

> The mother eagle wrecks her nest
> To make her fledglings fly,
> But watches each with outstretched wings
> And fierce maternal eye;
> And swoops, if any fails to soar,
> And lands them on the crag once more.
>
> So God at times breaks up our nest,
> *Lest, sunk in slothful ease,*
> *Our souls' wings moult, and lose the zest*
> *For battle with the breeze;*
> But ever waits with arms of love,
> To bear our souls all ills above.
>
> Anonymous

At a time of unwelcome disturbance, the author found this paragraph from a sermon of Samuel Chadwick both salutary and stimulating: "We are moved by the act of God. Omniscience holds no conference. Infinite authority leaves no room for compromise. Eternal love offers no explanations. The Lord expects to be trusted. He disturbs us at will. Human arrangements are disregarded, family ties ignored, business claims put aside. We are never asked if it is convenient."

Left in the comfortable nest, the eaglet's wings would never gain the strength to ascend in the face of the sun. Left in undisturbed comfort and prosperity, it is easy for *our* soul's wings to molt, and we lose the zest for spiritual conflict. Such disciplines fit us for the flight upward.

THE DISCIPLINE OF DARKNESS

The believer is nowhere promised that life will be all sunshine for him. Nor is he granted immunity, because he is a child of God, from "the slings and arrows of outrageous fortune." Land that knows nothing but sunshine becomes a desert. Clouds, storms, and darkness must have their place if there is to be fertility and fruitfulness.

In His wisdom and love, God sometimes allows us to pass through a period of unrelieved darkness, with no rift in the clouds. We seem to be in a tunnel with no ray of light at the end. Sometimes we are conscious that it is the result of our sin, and for that we can see some justification. But at other times, we are mystified because we cannot assign a reason for such an experience.

But it is not purposeless. "I will give you the treasures of darkness, and hidden wealth of secret places," is the divine assurance (Isa. 45:3). There are treasures to be won in such an experience that we can gain in no other way. Although the darkness may be thick, we can be sure that it is "the thick darkness where God was" (Exod. 20:21, NIV). Although we may not be able to descry His face in the darkness, if we stretch out the timid hand of faith, we will feel His reassuring clasp. "I am the LORD . . . I will also hold you by the hand" (Isa. 42:6).

A gifted missionary writer, whose life was both fragrant and fruitful, confided to the author that all her life she had to wage constant battle against depression—but one would never have dreamed it. She had garnered "the treasures of darkness."

The discipline of darkness was not absent from the experience of our Lord. Far deeper than the physical darkness that kindly shrouded His dying agonies was the darkness of soul that engulfed Jesus when His Father averted His face while He was expiating the sins of the world. Words of desolation were wrung from Him—"MY GOD, MY GOD, WHY HAST THOU FORSAKEN ME?"(Matt. 27:46) In the impenetrable gloom, although there was no single ray of light, His faith did not waver. His Father was still His God—"MY" God. Did He recall in that dark hour Isaiah's words; "Who is among you that fears the LORD, that obeys the voice of His servant, that walks in darkness and has no light? Let him trust in the name of the LORD and rely on his God" (50:10). Here is our pattern when we are in the midst of discipline. The rift in the clouds will come, the tunnel will end, and the test can be shortened when we react to it in a mature way. Then we will emerge, knowing an intimacy with God deeper than ever before. Was it not thus for the three young men when they emerged from Nebuchadnezzar's fiery furnace?

THE DISCIPLINE OF DISAPPOINTMENT

God nowhere undertakes to gratify our every whim or desire—only those that are according to His will and in our best interests. That is the reason that at times He seems unsympathetic toward something we think to be good. The mystery deepens when our desire appears to be for the glory of God. We should regard it as axiomatic that when God withholds some desired boon, it is only because He desires to bestow something He knows to be better.

> Let Him lead thee blindfold onwards,
>   Love needs not to know;
> Children whom the father leadeth
>   Ask not where they go
> Though the path be all unknown
> Over moors and mountains lone.
>
> Gerhard Tersteegen

Many have longed to do something worthy of the Lord they love, and their plans have seemed so right. But their desire has been thwarted. They desired to go to the mission field, but the door was closed by illness. They purposed to give generously to God's work but suffered financial reverses. They planned to train for Christian service, but family responsibilities intervened and made it impossible. Instead, they were faced with inactivity for activity, silence for speaking, obscurity for opportunity.

We should remember that for every disappointing "thou shalt not," there is a compensating "thou shalt." When we accept the divine discipline in a mature way, we will find that "some better thing" awaits us round the corner. We should learn to sing:

> I worship Thee, sweet will of God,
> And all Thy ways adore,
> And every day I live I seem
> To love Thee more and more.
>
> F. W. Faber

THE DISCIPLINE OF INEQUALITY

"The way of the Lord is not right," complained the Jews in Ezekiel's day (Ezek. 18:25). The same sentiments are echoed in our own times. Some feel they have been unfairly treated by God, and although they may never have expressed it in words, they feel disillusioned in their hearts, or cherish a secret resentment against Him. There is no simple answer to the question of why God intervenes in some cases and not in others, or spares one and not another. Why, when James was in prison did God allow him to be beheaded, while Peter was delivered by an angel and conducted to a prayer meeting? The only answer is, "You do not realize now what I am doing, but later you will understand"—that is sufficient for faith.

Such was the experience of Asaph the psalmist. When he saw the way in which wicked men prospered, while upright men seemed to experience more than their fair share of trial and trouble, he almost lost his faith. To what purpose was his endeavor to live a holy life when the wicked had all the best of things? Thoroughly disillusioned, he cried in his distress: "But for me, my feet came close to stumbling; my steps had almost slipped. . . . Until I came into the sanctuary of God . . ." (Psalm 73:2, 17).

In the presence of God, when he saw things from the divine perspective, faith returned. "Then I perceived their end," or final destiny (v. 17).

It is the end that is important, for there is a life beyond, where every inequality will be remedied; the wicked will receive the just consequences of their deeds and the righteous their due reward. The trouble is that we do not always repair to the sanctuary with our troubles. We correctly interpret a situation only when we turn from the immediate to the ultimate.

If ever anyone underwent the discipline of inequality, it was Job. He was described by the Almighty with glowing eulogy to Satan: "Have you considered My servant Job? For there is no one like him on the earth, a blameless and upright man, fearing God and turning away from evil" (Job 1:8). Here was a man who was on intimate terms with God. How does God treat the blameless and upright man? Surely he will be rewarded for his piety by special treatment and exemptions from trial.

The reverse was the case. He lost flocks, herds, servants, children, health, and , finally, the sympathy of his wife. Out of concern for her husband in his bitter trials, she urged him, "Curse God and die!"

"You speak as one of the foolish women speaks," was his rejoinder. "Shall we indeed accept good from God and not accept adversity?" (2:9-10)

He had already expressed his acceptance of the divine sovereignty in the words, "The LORD gave and the LORD has taken away. Blessed be the name of the LORD" (1:21). Job's reactions were those of a mature man of God. His intimacy with God enabled him to stand in the evil day. His steadfast loyalty to God silenced Satan in his design to discredit God. Job's reaction was not that of cold fatalism but of sublime faith. When the challenge came, he had his answer ready.

Job was totally unaware of the hidden issues behind his trials. He did not realize that he was the focal center of a contest between Satan and God, and that God had staked His confidence on Job's loyalty and integrity. Though he did not know it, his victory was a victory for his God; a victory all the greater because he was unaware of the issues at stake. And who knows what spiritual issues may be at stake when we are undergoing trial? Our reactions, observed by others, may have eternal implications, and may change the direction of other lives.

Amy Wilson Carmichael, the noble missionary who knew more than most of the experience of suffering and triumph over it, once said that she could not recall a single explanation of trial. We are trusted with the unexplained.

> The ills we see—
> The mysteries of sorrow deep and long
> The dark enigmas of permitted wrong—
> Have all one key
> The strange, sad world is but our Father's School
> All change and chance His love shall grandly overrule.
>
> Frances Ridley Havergal

The Discipline of Delay

On one occasion the Boston preacher Phillips Brooks was visited by a friend, who found him pacing up and down the room in great agitation.

"What's the matter, Phillips?" he asked.

"Matter enough," was the reply. "I am in a hurry and God is not."

Against the senseless and furious rush of our times, God often seems unduly leisurely in His intervention in our affairs. We want an answer, and we want it at once. But God does not always oblige. He refuses to be stampeded into premature action.

Our urgency and impatience stem from the shortness of our vision and the imperfection of our knowledge of all the facts. God's seeming leisureliness arises from His perfect knowledge of all the facts and His perfect control of all the circumstances. Nor does He always explain His tardiness.

Abraham, at his wife's suggestion, endeavored to advance the divine timetable. Through that act of unbelief, the Muslim scourge was unleashed on the world, and, indirectly, the price of gasoline has been pushed up! God will not be hurried. His delays are not capricious but purposeful.

The home of Bethany was always a restful haven for Jesus in the midst of His demanding journeys. On one occasion, while He was in the north of the land, Lazarus fell ill, and his sisters sent Jesus an urgent message, telling of their plight. They naturally expected that their Friend who had cured so many others would hurry at once to their side. Instead, when "He heard that [Lazarus] was sick, He stayed then two days longer in the place where He was" (John 11:6).

Further, in telling His disciples that Lazarus was dead, He actually said, "I am glad . . . I was not there" (v. 15). It was not that it afforded Him pleasure to refrain from rushing to His friends' side in their sorrow, but that they and His disciples might have an immeasurably more wonderful blessing and experience. His love for them was undoubted (v. 5). It was for their sakes He was glad, not His own. He was educating their faith—"So that you may believe" (v. 15). He had the same objective in view for Mary and Martha (v. 40).

In the event, though Jesus did not rush to their side, He did something much better. He will not spare present grief if it means future, permanent profit. He is concerned with our ultimate blessing more than our present comfort. But that does not mean that He is unmoved by our sorrows and trials.

> Think not thou canst sigh a sigh
> And Thy Maker is not by;

> Think not thou canst weep a tear
> And thy Maker is not near.
>
> William Blake

In subsequent days how often would the Bethany family repeat His statement: "We are glad that He was not here." For them and for His other disciples, He had become an infinitely greater Figure—One who was the resurrection and the life.

Those are some of the disciplines a loving Father employs to mature and lead us into a yet more intimate fellowship with Himself. It remains for us to react maturely to them.

Notes

1. V. R. Edman, *The Disciplines of Life* (Minneapolis: Worldwide Publications, 1948), p. 79.

It is more than comforting to realize that it is those who have plumbed the depth of failure to whom invariably God gives the call to shepherd others. This is not a call given to the gifted, the highly trained or the polished, as such.

Without a bitter experience of their own inadequacy and poverty, they are quite unfitted to bear the burden of spiritual ministry. It takes a man who had discovered something of the measures of his own weakness to be patient with the foibles of others. Such a man also has a firsthand knowledge of the loving care of the Chief Shepherd, and His ability to heal one who has come humbly to trust in Him and Him alone. [1]

J. C. Metcalfe

12

Intimacy Qualifies for a Ministry

Mark 10:31-45

In His memorable private interview with Peter after his denial, the Lord made it clear to His now deeply penitent friend that in the future the basis of their relations was to be unwavering devotion to Himself. For that there was no substitute. Three times He probed Peter's conscience to its depths with the searching query, "Simon, son of John, do you love Me?" (John 21:15-17) He knew that if Peter gave Him his unqualified love and devotion, he could then be entrusted as undershepherd, with the sensitive task of strengthening his brethren. Increasing intimacy would develop only through growing love.

Paul's experience of intimacy with Christ only fed the flames of a passion to know Him still better. "That I may know Him, and the power of His resurrection and the fellowship of His sufferings, being conformed to His death" (Phil. 3:10).

Paul had been assuring the believers at Philippi that his deepest concern was not his ancestry, achievements, or prestige, but the attaining of a deeper fellowship with his Lord. "But whatever things were gain to me, those things I have counted as loss for the sake of Christ. More than that, I count all things to be loss in view of the surpassing value of knowing Christ Jesus my Lord, for whom I have suffered the loss of all things, and count them but rubbish in order that I may gain Christ" (Phil. 3:7-8). For such an inestimable boon, no price was too great.

All spiritual ministry flows from the reality of our knowledge of God and the vitality of our fellowship with Him and His Son. A successful, fruitful ministry does not just happen—it is purchased. And the more influential the ministry, the steeper the price. It cannot be paid in a lump sum; we pay for it in gradually increasing installments. There is no such thing as a cheap, fruitful ministry.

Our Lord made it unequivocally clear that fruitfulness in service was inevitably linked with a cross: "Truly, truly, I say to you, unless a grain of wheat falls into the earth and dies, it remains by itself alone; but if it dies, it bears much fruit" (John 12:24). In that indisputable fact lies the explanation of the fruitfulness or the unfruitfulness of our lives. To the extent in which the cross is operative in our lives, will we live again in other lives. Did not the one kernel of wheat that fell into the ground at Calvary live again in three thousand lives on the day of Pentecost?

"Except it fall into the ground and die . . ."
    Can "much fruit" come alone at such a cost?
Must the seed corn be buried in the earth,
    All summer joy and glory seemingly lost?

"Except it fall into the ground and die . . ."
    But what a harvest in the days to come;
When fields stand thick with golden sheaves of corn
    And you are sharing in the Harvest Home.
To you who "lose your life," and let it die,
    Yet in the losing find your life anew,
Christ evermore unveils His lovely face,
    And thus His mirrored glory rests on you.

                                                    Anonymous

It should be understood that there is no shortcut to an influential ministry for God. James and John, by means of intrigue, endeavored to take one, but it proved a complete cul-de-sac (Mark 10:31). There may be shortcuts to ecclesiastical eminence or administrative authority, but not to a spiritual ministry. "True intimacy with anyone, most of all God, is not a thing that can be assumed at will: it is the outcome alone of dwelling in the secret place of the Most High, and abiding under the shadow of Shaddai."[2]

There is something to be said, however, in favor of James and John. At least they had believed in the Master's integrity in promising them that "in the regeneration when the Son of Man will sit on His glorious throne, you also shall sit upon twelve thrones, judging the twelve tribes of Israel" (Matt. 19:28). But they made the mistake of interpreting that statement in a temporal setting. Further, their surreptitious approach to Jesus evidenced an attempt to steal a march on their friends, by preempting the two most important offices in the Kingdom. They had carried over their craving for position and power from worldly standards of greatness. They coveted the crown—but without the thorns.

But Jesus would have none of it. There must be no pulling of strings to secure office in His Kingdom. Worldly principles and procedures of leadership must not be carried over. "You know that those who are recognized as rulers of the Gentiles lord it over them; and their great men exercise authority over them. But it is *not so among you*" (Mark 10:42-43, italics added).

SOVEREIGNTY IN A SPIRITUAL MINISTRY

In answer to their selfishly ambitious request, Jesus informed them, "To sit on My right or on My left, this is not Mine to give; but it is for those for whom it has been prepared" (10:40). Such positions were not automatically given to those who had prepared themselves, necessary and praiseworthy though that may be. The initiative is solely with God. No Bible or theological training, no leadership or church management course, no ordination service will per se confer a spiritual ministry. God will give those places to those for whom He has prepared them (v. 40).

We do not choose our own ministry. "You did not choose Me, but I chose you," declared the Lord (John 15:16). It is for us to discover from God the type and sphere of ministry He has prepared for us, and He will not fail to guide the genuine seeker. What assurance and rest of heart it brings when we can say with scriptural support, "I am here in this position not merely by the selection of a man or the election of a committee, but by the direct appointment of God."

SUFFERING IN A SPIRITUAL MINISTRY

Jesus was too honest and sincere to conceal from His disciples that often a spiritual ministry is costly. He desired them to follow Him, but with eyes wide open. So He challenged them: "You do not know what you are asking for. Are you able to drink the cup that I drink, or to be baptized with the baptism with which I am baptized?" (Mark 10:38) He would have them face up to the fact that while there was glory in following Him, it would not be all glory. They must learn that if they were to know Him more intimately, it would involve fellowship with Him in His sufferings. Their glib answer, "We are able" (v. 39), revealed their tragic lack of self-knowledge and unwarranted self-confidence.

James and John coveted positions of influential leadership but wanted them to come cheaply. Jesus told them that they would indeed drink the cup and experience the baptism (v. 39). In the end, James was executed, and John ended his days in a concentration camp on the Island of Patmos. A spiritual ministry is costly, and the path for the Master is the path for the servant.

The lesson for us is that if it is our inflexible purpose to spurn mediocrity and win through to an effective ministry, there will be a steep price to pay. But it will prove gloriously worthwhile.

Before he was qualified to lead God's people out of Egyptian bondage, Moses had to undertake postgraduate training. For forty years he had enjoyed luxurious living in a palace and education in Egypt's famous university. He was "educated in all the learning of the Egyptians, and he was a man of power in words and deeds" (Acts 7:22). There his intellect was sharpened and his social life polished, fitting him for ministry to the upper classes. But God's plan for him was the leadership of a nation of slaves. For that, further preparation was needed, the time in the bleak, barren desert. In that university, his spirit was tempered. In the unhurried solitude of his enforced isolation, he had abundant time to cultivate intimacy with God. Up until his desert experience, Moses had been an activist. Now he had to master a lesson very difficult to an activist—that *being* is more important than *doing*.

Paul had a somewhat similar experience. He pursued his academic studies under the tutelage of the famous Jewish rabbi, Gamaliel, gaining his Ph. D—Doctor of Pharisaism, someone has facetiously suggested. But though he had received superb academic training, he too had to retreat into solitude where his fiery spirit could be tempered, and he could undergo necessary theological orientation. "I did not immediately consult with flesh and blood," he claimed, "nor did I go up to Jerusalem to those who were apostles before me; but I went away into Arabia, and returned once more to Damascus. Then three years later I went up to Jerusalem" (Gal. 1:18). Three years alone with God in unbroken intimacy! What a preparation for spiritual ministry!

One important lesson to be learned from the experience of those men is that in training a man for a ministry, God does not shorten the training days, as we so often wish to do. For both, Moses and Paul a prolonged period of solitude was an important ingredient in their preparation and a necessary part of the maturing process.

Spiritual leadership does not always develop best in the limelight. There must be time for a future leader's secret transactions with God and for getting to know Him more intimately than do those he is being trained to lead. Because God is seeking quality in our lives, time is no object to Him.

SERVANTHOOD IN A SPIRITUAL MINISTRY

Jesus enunciated the revolutionary master principle for spiritual leadership: "Whoever wishes to become great among you shall be your servant; and whoever wishes to be first among you shall be slave of all. For even the Son of Man did not come to be served, but to serve, and to give His life a ransom for many" (Mark 10:43-45). He knew that would not be popular, for it cuts right across our cultural background and self-interest. Like James and John, most of us are very willing to be masters and wield authority, but we are not so willing to become everyone's slave.

Although our society has a very lowly estimate of servanthood, our Servant Lord elevated the concept and equated it with greatness. He did not discourage a desire to be *great* when it was inspired by worthy motives. What He castigated was the carnal ambition to be *greatest*.

In His statement, Jesus used two different words for "servant." The first was the general term, and refers to activity rather than to relationship. The second is the word for "bond-slave," and a slave is one who has no rights whatsoever over himself but belongs entirely to his master. It was that title that Paul appropriated to himself—"bond-servant of Christ Jesus" (Rom. 1:1).

The relevant background is found in Exodus 21:1-6 where the ideal relationship between slave and master in Old Testament times is foreshadowed. Paul's attitude is reflected in Frances Ridley Havergal's hymn based on that passage:

> I love, I love my Master,
> I will not go out free,

For He is my Redeemer;
He paid the price for me.
I would not leave His service,
It is so sweet and blest;
And in the weariest moments
He gives the truest rest.

From those considerations there emerges the fact that the criterion by which we are to judge our spiritual ministry is not the number of servants who minister to our needs, but the number of people whom we serve. Increasing intimacy with Him who said, "I am among you as the one who serves" (Luke 22:27), will mean that we will partake progressively of His spirit of service.

Only once did Jesus say to His disciples that He was leaving them an example, and that was when He "laid aside His garments; and taking a towel, girded Himself about. Then He poured water into the basin, and began to wash the disciples' feet, and to wipe them with the towel with which He was girded"(John 13:4-5). *An example of servanthood!*

There is only one place in the New Testament where He is said by others to have left an example. "Christ also suffered for you, leaving you an example for you to follow in His steps" (1 Pet. 2:21). *An example of suffering.*

He thus underlined the searching fact that essential elements of a spiritual ministry are servanthood and suffering.

Notes

1. Miles J. Stanford, *Principles of Spiritual Growth* (Lincoln: Back to the Bible, 1977), p. 28.
2. W. Graham Scroggie, *Method in Prayer* (London: Hodder & Stoughton, 1916), pp. 125-26.

I would emphasize this one committal, this one great volitional act which establishes the heart's intention to gaze forever upon Jesus. God takes this intention for our choice and makes what allowances He must for the thousand distractions which beset us in this evil world. He knows that we have set the direction of our hearts toward Jesus, and we can know it too, and comfort ourselves with the knowledge that a habit of soul is forming which will become after a while a sort of spiritual reflex requiring no more conscious effort on our part. [1]

A. W. Tozer

13

Intimacy Produces Spiritual Maturity

Ephesians 4:11-16

There are few more attractive sights than that of an increasingly intimate friendship and fellowship developing between a father and his son, as the latter matures into adulthood. A growing mutual appreciation and a sharing in increasing depth of thought and experience mark their communication. Each enjoys the other.

It is that kind of relationship that God desires to sustain with His children as they progress toward maturity. Just as the caring parent delights to observe a child developing an all-around maturity of character, so God rejoices to see in His children a growing likeness to His Son—the only perfectly mature Man. Such maturity opens the door to an ever-deepening intimacy, and, in turn, that intimacy makes possible and accelerates a greater maturity of spiritual life and character.

WHAT IS SPIRITUAL MATURITY?

The Greek word for "maturity"—teleios—"an end, or goal, or limit," is rich in its significance. It combines two ideas: (a) the attaining of some standard, and (b) the achieving of some goal. Of the use of the word in Matthew 5:48, A. T.

Robertson says, "Here it is the goal set before us, the absolute standard of our heavenly Father. The word is used also for relative perfection, as of adults compared with children."[2]

As Paul used the word, it meant "brought to completion, full-grown, lacking nothing." In writing to the Christians at Ephesus, he informed them that the gifted men whom the Spirit had given to the church had their function, "for the equipping of the saints for the work of service, to the building up of the body of Christ; until we all attain to the unity of the faith, and of the knowledge of the Son of God, to a *mature man*, to the measure of the stature which belongs to the fulness of Christ. As a result, we are *no longer to be children . . .* we are to *grow up* in all aspects into Him, who is the Head, even Christ" (4:12-15, italics added).

Note the emphasis—becoming mature, ceasing to be children, growing up. And the standard by which maturity is to be measured is clearly stated—"the measure of the stature which belongs to the fulness of Christ." What will the mature Christian be like? He will be like Christ. Spiritual maturity, expressed in the simplest terms, is—*Christlikeness*. We are mature only insofar as we are like Him. That concept is borne out by the fact that, when we attain full maturity at Christ's second advent, "we shall be like Him, because we shall see Him just as He is" (1 John 3:2).

In the Ephesian passage, the apostle links our maturity with "the knowledge of the Son of God" (4:13). To know Him more fully and deeply is an essential factor in attaining maturity, and that is necessarily a progressive thing, for we are exhorted to "grow in the . . . knowledge of our Lord and Savior Jesus Christ" (2 Pet. 3:18). Ideally, we begin our spiritual lives as babes in Christ; then we progress through spiritual adolescence; finally we attain to a mature adult status. That fundamental pattern of life and growth prevails in the spiritual as well as in the physical realm.

DEGREES OF MATURITY

The apostle John, in his first letter, recognized this fact when he addressed himself to his readers as little children, fathers, and young men (1 John 2:12-14). He took note of the fact that there are different stages of growth in the Christian life, attained by different students in the school of Christ.

The important thing is that we must "press on to maturity" (Heb. 6:1). Keep on growing. Too many Christians become stuck in their Christian lives —"stuck between Easter and Pentecost," as Dr. Graham Scroggie put it.

A godly Christian lady known to the author was dying of cancer. She knew she had only a few days to live. Her husband was attending to her needs, trying to make things as easy as possible for her. She said to him, "You must not make things too easy for me. I must keep growing, you know." Her life of intimacy with God had brought her to a state of spiritual maturity in which she was more concerned about growing up into Christ than about her own very real pain and discomfort. We too need to be ambitious to increase in our knowledge of God.

The writer of the letter to the Hebrews urged his readers to cultivate such an ambition, in these words: "Therefore leaving the elementary teaching about the Christ, let us press on to maturity" (6:1). Dr. Alexander Smellie pointed out that the King James Version renders it, "Let us go on." The Revised Version renders it, "Let us press on." Bishop Westcott prefers to render it, "Let us be borne on."

"The truth is that it needs all three to disclose the verb's significance and wealth. Put them together, and they speak to us of three dangers which beset us as we look to the perfection front. There is the danger of stopping too soon. There is the danger of sinking into discouragement. And there is the danger of supposing that we are alone."[3] How gracious God is to make provision through the ministry of the Holy Spirit, for our being "borne on to maturity."

Paul tells us further, in his second letter to the Corinthians, how the maturing process may be accelerated. "But we all, with unveiled face beholding as in a mirror the glory of the Lord, are being transformed into the same image from glory to glory, just as from the Lord, the Spirit" (2 Cor. 3:18).

"You would be like Christ?" asked Andrew Murray. "Here is the path. Gaze on the glory of God in Him. *In Him*, that is to say, do not look only to the words and the thoughts and the graces in which His glory is seen, but look to Himself, the loving, living Christ. Behold Him! Look in His very eye! Look into His face, as a loving friend, as the living God."[4]

THE TRANSFORMING VISION

The transformation into Christ's likeness begins, as 2 Corinthians 3:18 indicates, not with subjective introspection, but with the objective vision of the glory of the Lord as it was manifested in Jesus. That captivating vision is to be seen not in illuminated heavens, but in the written Word of God, illumined by the inspiring Spirit. The Word is a mirror that reveals and reflects Christ's unique character, perfect manhood, flawless character, and redemptive work. God has thus made His light to shine "in our hearts to give the light of the knowledge of the glory of God in the face of Christ" (2 Cor. 4:6).

The glory of God is not abstract or ethereal; it was actually revealed in terms of human life, in the person and work of Christ. But where can we see authoritatively the face of Jesus Christ? Not on the artist's canvas, for his portrait is but the projection of his own ideas and concepts. Christ's face may be seen in the word pictures painted for us in such beautiful colors by the gospel biographers who, under the inspiration of the Spirit, present us with a full length portrait of Him. The Jews of His day saw the face, but missed the glory, because their prejudice and unbelief concealed it more impenetrably than the veil that hid the glory on Moses' face when he returned from talking with God (Exod. 34:33-35).

An objective vision of the glory of God will effect a subjective transformation in those who gaze upon it. An unknown author has expressed that truth:

> Show me Thy face—one transient gleam
>   Of loveliness divine,
> And I shall never think or dream
>   Of other love save Thine:
> All lesser light will darken quite,
>   All lower glories wane,
> The beautiful of earth will scarce
>   Seem beautiful again.
>
> Show me Thy face—my faith and love
>   Shall henceforth fixed be,
> And nothing here have power to move
>   My soul's serenity.
> My life shall seem a trance, a dream,
>   And all I feel and see,
> Illusive, visionary—Thou
>   The one reality!

God's purpose for His children is not external imitation, but internal transformation. The glory that was seen on Moses' face when he descended from the mountain was evanescent and fading. But the glory of which Paul is here speaking is a glory *retained and transmitted,* for the word rendered "beholding" here may equally be rendered "reflecting."

THE METHOD OF TRANSFORMATION

The method by which that transformation is effected is not "a despairing struggle against that which captivates," but a steady, consistent "beholding"—gazing on Christ in all His majesty, glory, love, holiness, truth, and justice, as those are set forth in Scripture. It is while we are beholding them that we are being changed into His likeness.

The eye exercises a powerful influence on Christian character. We become like those whom we admire. Alexander the Great read Homer's *Iliad* and set out to conquer the world. Character and habits are molded by the manners and habits of those whom we are constantly seeing. Who has not seen pale imitations of famous movie stars parading the streets?

How does the Holy Spirit effect such radical change in us? There is a parallel on the physical level in the ingestion and digestion of food. We eat our meal and forget all about it. Our bodily functions and gastric juices take over, and without any conscious volition or activity on our part, the food is gradually changed into another form and is incorporated into the texture of our physical bodies. It is changed into flesh, bone, blood, hair, and energy. And all without any conscious action on our part.

Similarly as we spend time devoutly "beholding . . . the glory of the Lord" in the face of Jesus Christ—His virtues, graces, achievements—the Holy Spirit not only *reveals* Him to us, but He *reproduces* Him in us. Without conscious volition on our part, He incorporates into the fabric of our spiritual lives the virtues and values we see in Christ, and transforms us increasingly into His likeness. "Beholding . . . the glory of the Lord, [we] are being transformed into the same image" (2 Cor. 3:18).

Our transformation is progressive, for it is "from glory to glory."

> Changed from glory into glory
> Till in heaven we take our place,
> Till we cast our crowns before Thee
> Lost in wonder, love and praise.
>
> Charles Wesley

The inward change is not the result merely of some moment of high and holy exaltation. It is as we continue gazing at Him that we are continually being transformed. There is no grace we see in glorious character of our Lord that may not be ours in increasing measure as we rely on the Holy Spirit to reproduce it in us.

So wrote A. W. Tozer:

> Many have found the secret of which I speak and, without giving much thought to what was going on within them, constantly practice this habit of inwardly gazing on God. They know that something inside their hearts sees God. Even when they are compelled to withdraw their conscious attention in order to engage in earthly affairs, there is within them a secret communion going on. Let their attention be released but for a moment from necessary business, and it flies to God once again.[5]

Our part is *to behold*. The Spirit's prerogative is to *transform*.

Notes

1. A. W. Tozer, *The Pursuit of God* (India: Alliance Publications, 1967), p. 82.
2. A. T. Robertson, *Word Pictures in the New Testament* (New York: Harpers, 1930), p. 49.
3. W. H. G. Thomas, *Let Us Go On* (Chicago: Moody, n.d.) p. 69.
4. Andrew Murray, *Like Christ* (London: J. Nisbet, n.d.) p. 148.
5. Tozer, ibid., p. 87.

*What is Christ's claim upon us if we want to be His disciples?
First of all, a supreme love. We cannot follow Christ unless
we love Him better than anyone else. He puts Himself
alongside the dearest relationships of earth, and says in un-
forgettable words, "You must hate all these, or you cannot be
my disciple." . . . The word "hate" is a relative word; it is not
absolute. . . .*

*He demands from you and me a love greater than the earliest
love—the love to father and mother; greater than the dearest
love—the love to wife and child; greater than the nearest love—
the love of our own life.* [1]

W. Y. Fullerton

14

Intimacy Implies Discipleship

Luke 6:12-13

The twelve intimates of Jesus were called disciples, and disciples are pupils, or learners. Those men, who were privileged to enjoy three years of uninterrupted intimacy with the Son of God, constituted the foundation of the universal church He was to build. No men before or since have enjoyed so rare a privilege, but not until after the resurrection did they fully recognize its magnitude.

The selection of the men who would be crucial to the success of the whole enterprise was one of the critical points in our Lord's ministry. Recognizing that, before selecting them, "He spent the whole night in prayer to God. And when day came, He called His disciples to Him; and chose twelve of them" (Luke 6:12-13).

Several factors prompted Him to take action.

The hostility of the rulers was rising. "They themselves were filled with rage, and discussed together what they might do to Jesus" (Luke 6:11).

His popularity was increasing to such an extent that He was unable to exploit the opportunities that afforded, without the help of others. "And there was a great multitude of His disciples, and a great throng of people from all Judea, and Jerusalem and the coastal region of Tyre and Sidon, who had come to hear Him, and to be healed of their diseases" (Luke 6:17-18). The potential harvest demanded more reapers.

Further, *he craved human companionship*, for He was truly man. "We do not have a high priest who cannot sympathize with our weaknesses" (Heb. 4:15). He longed for some fellowship to take the place of what He had renounced, so He surrounded Himself with an inner circle of twelve.

Imperfect though they were, their devotion and love were very real and precious to Him. Their loyalty, faltering though it was, led Him to pay a moving tribute to them at the Last Supper: "You are those who have stood by Me in My trials" (Luke 22:28).

CRITERIA OF SELECTION

There is much for our comfort and instruction in the incident. As in so many things, the method of the Master ran counter to the normal pattern of the times. In the light of contemporary practice, there are some startling omissions from the categories from which He selected His men. Religious leaders and university professors were conspicuous by their absence. The aristocracy was not represented. Not one of the chosen twelve was wealthy, none had great social standing. There were no "stars" to add distinction to the group.

In Judaism it was the custom for the pupil to select the rabbi of his choice and attach himself to him for instruction. Thus Paul sat "at the feet of Gamaliel" (Acts 22:3, KJV). But here it was Jesus and not the disciples who took the initiative. "When day came, He called His disciples to Him; and chose twelve of them" (Luke 6:13). Later He reminded them, "You did not choose Me, but I chose you" (John 15:16). He called them personally and bound them to Him with bonds of affection that stood the test of time. Thus He chose to invest His life and channel it into that little group of men.

O mystery of grace,
That chooseth us to stand before Thy face,

To be Thy special measure,
Thy portion, Thy delight, Thine own;
    That taketh pleasure
In them that fear Thy name, that hope alone
In Thy sweet mercy's boundless store.

                              Frances Ridley Havergal

He purposefully did not choose them from the influential class, but from the humbler walks of life—fishermen, tradesmen, a taxgatherer. He chose men unspoiled by the sophistication of high society—simple, unaffected men. He chose artisans—of whom He Himself was one, men with little formal education and with no obvious special qualifications. Later, however, they proved to be skilled, resourceful, articulate men who could think, speak, and write effectively.

But why no scholars among them? Paul, Luke, and others were to follow later, but no intellectuals were numbered among our Lord's intimates. Was it because they would be less teachable, less willing to embrace the revolutionary principles He would enunciate?

They were "men of like passions," men just like us. They were not "impossible saints." They were not theologians or political leaders—just ordinary men who became extraordinary under the molding hand of the Master Potter. That makes His selection of them the more wonderful, for had He chosen all men who were intellectually brilliant, men of great spiritual stature, how could ordinary people be expected to aspire to a similar discipleship?

In order to shape and prepare them for the task of world evangelism, Jesus was willing to restrict His own privacy and liberty by living in close daily contact with them. He wanted not servants, but friends who would be sympathetically involved in assisting Him to fulfill the task He had come to do. They shared with Him the ordinary chores and cares of daily life. Unconsciously, under His gracious tuition, they began to absorb His teaching and imbibe His spirit.

Their imperfections were painfully apparent, but those did not debar them from His fellowship and friendship. If God required perfection before He admitted us into the circle of His fellowship, who would qualify? Quirks of temperament did not disqualify them, or Peter with his volatile nature would not have been counted in. Nor would James and John with their selfish ambition and callous racism. Thomas's disbelief would have placed him outside the circle. But Jesus welcomed them all into the circle of His love and intimacy. "Having loved His own who were in the world, He now showed them the full extent of His love" (John 13:1 NIV).

TERMS OF DISCIPLESHIP

Having selected His men, Jesus proceeded to make clear to them, as they were able to bear it, the implications of their discipleship. He was too caring and honest to conceal from them the fact that the road ahead of them would not be primrose-strewn. He wanted men to follow Him with eyes wide open. Browning correctly interpreted His mood when he wrote:

> How very hard it is to be a Christian!
> Hard for you and me;
> Not the mere task of making real
> That duty up to its ideal,
> Effecting, thus complete and whole,
> A purpose of the human soul—
>
> For that is always hard to do;
> But hard, I mean, for me and you
> To realize it, more or less,
> With even the moderate success
> Which commonly repays our strife
> To carry out the aims of life.

Sometimes He taught them those principles by direct statement; at other times by parables. Among the principles He enjoined, these were prominent:

CONTINUANCE IN HIS WORD

"Jesus therefore was saying to those Jews who had believed Him, 'If you abide in My word, then you are truly disciples of Mine' " (John 8:31). Only thus can intimacy develop.

"How does God reveal what has to be revealed in order to know Him?" asks J. I. Packer.

> By verbal communication from Himself. . . . God reveals Himself by telling us about Himself, and what He is doing in the world. . . .
>
> Why does God reveal Himself to us? Because He who made us rational beings wants, in His love, to have us as His friends; and He addresses His words to us—statements, commands, promises—as a means of sharing His thoughts with us, and so of making that personal self-disclosure which friendship presupposes, and without which it cannot exist. [2]

What did Jesus mean by His "word"? It would seem that He was referring to the sum and substance of all that He taught, the whole content of His teaching. That idea is caught in the NIV translation of John 8:31: "If you hold to My teaching, you are really My disciples." To continue in His teaching simply means to make it the rule of life. Our continuance in it will be the test of the reality of our discipleship.

Paul exhorted the Colossian Christians: "Let the word of Christ richly dwell within you" (Col. 3:16). Dwelling in His Word will involve devout meditation, serious study, and loyal obedience. As we live in it, we will gain a widening grasp of the spiritual principles by which we are to live and grow.

OBEDIENCE TO HIS COMMANDS

In His Sermon on the Mount, Jesus asked the searching question: "Why do you call Me, 'Lord, Lord,' and do not do what I say?" (Luke 6:46) Mere profession of friendship and love is not enough. Their obedience would be the evidence of their discipleship. There can be no reserved areas.

Of all His commands, the command to love is the greatest,

and obedience to it would mean that "all men will know that you are My disciples" (John 13:35). Jesus Himself was their model, for He said, "Even as I have loved you, that you also love one another" (John 13:34).

That commandment has special reference to the love Christians should bear toward fellow Christians. The commandment itself was not new. The new element was that that mutual affection among Christians was to be on account of and inspired by Christ's greater love for them.

How deeply Jesus loved His men! To what lengths His love carried Him! Even base betrayal did not quench His efforts to bring the traitor back into the inner circle of His fellowship. "Immediately [Judas] came to Jesus and said, 'Hail, Rabbi!' and kissed Him. And Jesus said to him, '*Friend*, do what you have come for' " (Matt. 26:49-50, italics added).

Though Peter had cravenly denied Him among His enemies, the Master's chief concern was to restore the love relationship that had been ruptured. So He appointed a special rendezvous and sent a special message to him. When they met, the Lord's reiterated question was, "Simon, son of John, do you love Me?" (John 21:16) He restored Simon Peter to the apostolate and entrusted him with new responsibilities. But best of all, He admitted him once again into the inner circle.

Notes

1. W. Y. Fullerton, *Keswick Week 1915* (London: Marshalls, 1915), p. 29.
2. J. I. Packer, *God Has Spoken* (London: Hodder & Stoughton, 1968), pp. 80-81.

Paul has now supplied several reasons for his refusal to grow discouraged in spite of seemingly overwhelming odds: his divine commission as a minister of a new and superior covenant, the prospect of sharing Christ's triumphant resurrection from the dead, and his immediate task of promoting the Corinthians' spiritual welfare and the glory of God.

But Paul was realistic enough to recognize that his toil and suffering had taken their toll physically. For this however, there was a splended compensation. Matching the progressive weakening of his physical powers, was the daily renewal of his spiritual powers. It was as though the more he expended, the greater his spiritual resilience. [1]

Murray J. Harris

15

Intimacy Prevents Discouragement

2 Corinthians 4:1, 16; 5:6, 8

Paul was writing to the Christians at Corinth about the glory of the ministry of the New Covenant and cited Moses' experience on Mount Sinai when "his face shone because of his speaking with [the LORD]" (Exod. 34:29). He shared with them the secret of sharing and reflecting that radiance. "We, who with unveiled faces all reflect the Lord's glory, are being transformed into His likeness with ever increasing glory, which comes from the Lord who is the Spirit" (2 Cor. 3:18).

He then proceeded to show that those and other related truths are a sure preventative of discouragement. "Therefore, since we have this ministry, as we received mercy, *we do not lose heart*" (2 Cor. 4:1, italics added).

It was three o'clock in the morning. The preceding days had been filled with abnormal pressures. I was due to leave in two or three hours to speak at a conference of missionaries in an unusually difficult and unresponsive field. Many of them had become more than a little discouraged at the hardness of the way. There had been no time whatever for special preparation, but I felt I must have a message of encouragement to bring them from the Lord.

As sleep was impossible, I switched on the light and took up C. K. Williams' translation, *The New Testament in Plain*

English. Without design, it fell open at 2 Corinthians, chapters 4 and 5. Four sentences that had been underlined caught my eye: *"We do not lose heart"*; *"We are of good heart always"* (4:1, 16; 5:6, 8) I had my message.

Who of us has never been tempted to lose heart? Who has not been on the point of dropping his bundle? None of us is exempt from the subtle, debilitating attacks of our adversary on that level. Few are fortunate enough to escape periods of depression, whether as a result of adverse circumstances or the tyranny of temperament. That Paul had been no stranger to that malady of the soul is clear from his four-times repeated assertions, "We do not lose heart"; "We are of good heart always." But by the time he penned that letter, he had mastered the secret of endurance and victory.

It is a strong statement, and alternative translations highlight its meaning: "We never give up." "We don't get discouraged." "Nothing can daunt us." "We never collapse." There must of necessity be some very strong motivation, some unusual secret of power, that enabled Paul to make such a daring assertion.

"But that was the great apostle Paul," do you say? "If I were Paul with his spectacular gifts of nature and of grace, his superb training, his apostolic authority, and his success in service, perhaps I would not lose heart either. But I am no Paul!"

But did everything drop into Paul's lap? Was he spared the acute testings that beset a Christian worker or beleaguered missionary or pastor? On that morning, I quickly thumbed through Paul's second letter to the Corinthians to discover the kind of circumstances over which he triumphed. Pause here and read 1:8; 2:4; 4:8; 6:4-10; 7:5; 11:23-28; 12:7. What a mounting crescendo of trials! How trivial our burdens appear when compared to the weight of his cares.

It should be borne in mind that in those passages Paul shared with us the secrets of his victory over depression and discouragement. It is most unlikely that he reached that plane of victory all at once. He was not immune to depression, for did he not write, "But God, who comforts the depressed, comforted us by the coming of Titus" (2 Cor. 7:6)? He was not spared the normal educational and disciplinary experiences of life. *"I have learned,"* he wrote, "to be content in whatever circumstances I am" (Phil. 4:11, italics added).

> Discouraged in the work of life,
> Disheartened by its load,
> Shamed by its failures or its fears,
> I sink beside the road;
> But let me only think of Thee,
> And then new heart springs up in me.
>
> Samuel Longfellow

How did Paul rise above discouragement and never lose heart?

HE WAS ENTRUSTED WITH A MINISTRY

> Therefore, since we have this ministry as we received mercy, *we do not lose heart.* [2 Cor. 4:1, italics added]

We lose heart when we lose the sense of wonder at the surpassing superiority of the ministry entrusted to us. "We have been entrusted with this commission" (NEB*). We are not self-appointed or self-made men. "Our adequacy is from God, who also made us adequate as servants of a new covenant" (2 Cor. 3:5-6).

Paul was very conscious of the fact that his bitter persecution of the church had totally disqualified him for such a ministry. "I am the least of the apostles, who am not fit to be called an apostle, because I persecuted the church of God" (1 Cor. 15:9). But he had "received mercy" and, wonder of wonders, had been entrusted with the ministry of a New Covenant: *Therefore* . . . we do not lose heart" (italics added).

---

*New English Bible.

The message of the New Covenant was a revolutionary concept. At this distance, it is difficult for us to realize how utterly incredible it was to the Jews. It was an absolute reversal of the Old Covenant under which they had lived. The inexorable *"thou shalt"* of that covenant, with its relentless demand of an obedience that proved beyond the power of unaided man to render, becomes the reassuring *"I will"* of the New Covenant. Here was the promise of divine enabling, and better still, divine intimacy: "I will be their God, and they shall be My people" (Jer. 31:33).

The New Covenant is not a message directed to a spiritual elite, but is tailored to meet the needs of men and women who had utterly failed. It is a covenant for failures, in which Christ undertakes to be surety for them. It is based on the assurance that sin is forgiven and forgotten: "I WILL BE MERCIFUL TO THEIR INIQUITIES, AND I WILL REMEMBER THEIR SINS NO MORE" (Heb. 8:12). It holds out the promise that the Holy Spirit will impart the desire to do the will of God. "I will put My spirit within you, and cause you to walk in My statutes, and you will be careful to observe My ordinances" (Ezek. 36:27).

Having been entrusted with such a revolutionary message, Paul says, "No wonder we do not lose heart!"

He Was Endowed with New Strength

Therefore we do not lose heart. Though outwardly we are wasting away, yet inwardly we are being renewed day by day. [2 Cor. 4:16, Williams†, italics added]

Here Paul reviewed his soul-winning ministry with all the perils it involved and the burdens it imposed. Death was always an imminent possibility. Inevitably, in the midst of the wear and tear of his service and suffering, his outer man, his body, was wearing away. But that was not the whole story. A counterprocess was also taking place—his inner

†Charles B. Williams, *The New Testament, A Translation in the Language of the People.*

being was at the same time experiencing daily renewal. He was receiving fresh accessions of strength from God day by day. "No wonder we do not give up!" he exclaimed. Daily fellowship with God ensured daily spiritual renewal.

Paul did not receive from God special favors that were not available to his contemporaries and to us. True, he had gifts and abilities far above ours, but God has blessed us equally with him "with every spiritual blessing in the heavenly places in Christ" (Eph. 1:3). Then why the discrepancy between his experience and ours? Why are we so often weak and fail? Could it be because Paul daily appropriated, made his own, his share of the divine provision whereas we do not? Why do we not take more from God when He has made such ample provision for our daily needs?

Our Father knows the strains and stresses involved in daily life and service. He is not insensitive to its costliness or to the fact that "outwardly we are wasting away." He knows when we are nearing the point of collapse, and, to counteract that, He promises daily renewal.

What is involved in being "renewed"? Does it mean that we receive a fresh supply of resolution or courage? That may be part of it, but Paul speaks of having "put on the new self who is being renewed to a true knowledge according to the image of the One who created him" (Col. 3:10). It is a renewal after the image of the Creator and the result of a deepening knowledge of Him.

Paradoxically, in the process He uses the very affliction that is responsible for the decaying of the old man to effect an inward renewal that lifts us above the tyranny of the physical (2 Cor. 4:17). Paul lists other paradoxical experiences too, in this remarkable passage:

> The heavy burden is light.
> The ethereal glory is a weight.
> The seemingly endless period of trial is momentary.
> The momentary affliction brings eternal blessing.

And that powerful, inner renewal is available to us, not only in times of spiritual crisis, but "day by day," to enable us to meet and overcome the daily demands of life and service.

"No wonder we do not lose heart!"

HE WAS ENDUED WITH THE SPIRIT

It is God Himself who has made us ready for this change, and has given us the Spirit, a part-payment and promise of more. So we are of good heart always. [2 Cor. 5:5-6, Williams]

The expression here and in 5:8 is different from that in 4:1, 16, but it carries much the same meaning. It signifies to be cheerful and "of good courage." Was it Paul's circumstances that kept him always cheerful? We know the answer. It was not his circumstances, but the gift of the Comforter, One called alongside to strengthen and help. And what a Gift that is! Paul's joy and unshakable confidence had their source in the presence and ministry of the Holy Spirit in his heart and life. Because the Spirit was always present, always active, Paul could always be of good heart. With such a mighty indwelling Guest, despair and discouragement were unnecessary. To submit to them would be to dishonor the Spirit whose delight it was to maintain him in unbroken fellowship with his Lord.

Paul had in mind, too, that the gift of the Spirit, in which he had participated, was "a part-payment and promise of more." The highest and holiest experience of the Holy Spirit's ministry we have ever known is only a foretaste of more glorious possibilities ahead.

Because of the ceaseless activity of the Holy Spirit in his life and service, Paul felt he had every reason to be of good heart always.

HE WAS ENGROSSED WITH THE ETERNAL

We have to walk by faith, not by sight, but *we are in good heart,*

and are quite content to leave the body behind and go home to
the Lord. [2 Cor. 5:7-8, Williams, italics added]

Paul had just written, "While we look not at the things
which are seen, but at the things which are not seen; for the
things which are seen are temporal, but the things which are
not seen are eternal" (2 Cor. 4:18). For him death held no
terrors because he was mastered by the powers of the world
to come.

When our gaze is concentrated on the things around
us—political revolution, industrial chaos, economic instability, war, crime, violence, lawlessness, the diminishing sanc-
tity of marriage—there is much to discourage and little to
kindle optimism. But Paul exhorts us to lift our eyes and
become engrossed with eternal values. He reminds us that
the Christian is not to walk according to the dictates of sight
but by faith in the eternal and all-powerful God.

Peter looked at his Lord and triumphantly walked on the
unstable waves. When he shifted his gaze and became engrossed with the waves, he was engulfed. When will we
master that elementary lesson of the spiritual life?

There is one more occurrence of the expression we have
been considering:

HE WAS ENCOURAGED
BY THE ASSURANCE OF HARVEST

And let us not grow tired in doing right; for when the time
comes, *if we do not lose heart,* we shall reap. [Gal. 6:9, Williams,
italics added]

For a Christian worker there are few more fruitful causes of
discouragement and loss of heart than the lack of visible evidence of success. We give ourselves to our task without stint
or reservation. We pray and work and sometimes weep, and
yet the harvest tarries, and we tend to collapse. Our wily
adversary plays his cards shrewdly at such times, and often
we fail to detect his strategy and fall into his snare.

The time factor in Galatians 6:9 is important—"when the time comes." There is always an interval between sowing and reaping. The process of germination and maturation takes time and is largely invisible. But "when the time comes," the proper time, harvest is certain.

So let us not grow tired, and let us not lose heart, for "he who goes to and fro weeping, carrying his bag of seed, shall indeed come again with a shout of joy, bringing his sheaves with him" (Psalm 126:6).

Notes

1. Murray J. Harris, *Expositors' Bible Commentary* (Grand Rapids: Zondervan, 1976), p. 344.

The apostle John links money and the love of God: "But whoso hath this world's good, and seeth his brother have need, and shutteth up his heart from him, how dwelleth the love of God in him?" (1 John 3:17) This verse is preceded by one which says we ought to lay down our lives for the brethren, in order to give the ultimate proof of love, but of course most Christians will never have the opportunity to do this. . . . How then can the believer in ordinary circumstances show that he loves his brother and thus God? By giving money and goods to his brother. If he fails to do this, then he shows not only that he does not love his brother, but also that he does not love God. [1]

Charles C. Ryrie

16

Intimacy Begets Liberality

2 Corinthians 8:1-7

It would be impossible to experience increasing intimacy with the "God who richly supplies us with all things to enjoy" (1 Tim. 6:17) without expressing it in increasing likeness to Him in this respect. Fellowship with God means a growing oneness of viewpoint and action.

Jesus began His Sermon on the Mount with a string of eight beatitudes. To those He added a ninth, which is one of His few authentic sayings recorded outside the gospels: "It is more blessed to give than to receive" (Acts 20:35). God is a generous Giver, but not all of His children partake of His spirit and qualify for that beatitude.

WHAT DID JESUS PRACTICE?

Our Lord's life on earth as a man set the standard for His disciples, and this principle applies equally to living for God and giving to God. Paul holds Him up as the supreme Example. "You know the grace of our Lord Jesus Christ, that though He was rich, yet for your sake He became poor, that you through His poverty might become rich" (2 Cor. 8:9).

Judaism was an expensive religion, and as a devout Jew who fulfilled the whole Law, our Lord was meticulous in fulfilling its financial obligations. What would He pay into the Temple treasury from what He earned as a carpenter?

A Jew was first required to give one tenth to God. Then at harvest time, the farmer must give the firstfruits to God, and that consisted of one sixth of his increase. Then every three years a second tenth was given for the poor—social security tax. In addition were the special offerings of cleansing and consecration. That means that his total contributions to religion would be nearer a fifth of his income than a tenth—and that does not include voluntary support to the local synagogue.[2] It is not difficult to imagine the temptation in times of stringency to withhold the tithe. So here we have our answer as to how much of His income Jesus gave to God.

If we object that the Jews were under law and we Christians are under grace, and that for us the law of the tithe has been abrogated, another question arises. Will a Christian who is experiencing intimacy with his Lord wish to take advantage of grace so that he can give less to God's work than the less privileged Jew who knew nothing of Calvary's sacrifice and the inestimable blessings it has brought? Was our Lord's matchless generosity in becoming poor for us intended to beget parsimony in His children? Paul cited it rather as an incentive to sacrificial giving.

In speaking about tithing in Matthew 23:23, Jesus said, relevant:

Admittedly, tithing is nowhere specifically commanded in the New Testament, since that is not the genius of God's method under grace. Instead of legislating regulations, Jesus enunciated principles by which His disciples were to regulate their conduct. "I am not commanding you" were Paul's words. He knew that a lavish hand without a loving heart was valueless.

Tithing was practiced by the patriarchs four hundred years before the Law was given (Gen. 14:20; 28:22). The usage of consecrated tithes prevailed among Romans, Greeks, and Arabians as well as with the Jews; so tithing seems to rest on the common law of God's Kingdom rather than on special Hebrew legislation.

Jesus gave tithes and offerings. Is the servant greater than his Lord?

It is a misconception of the meaning of "grace" to think that it leaves it open for a believer to do less than a devout Jew would have done. If the true spirit of grace has gripped my heart, I will not be calculating the minimum I can get away with, but the maximum I can give to my Lord. The New Testament standard is not lower than the Old.

In speaking about tithing in Matthew 23:23, Jesus said, "You tithe mint and dill and cummin, and have neglected the weightier provisions of the law: justice and mercy and faithfulness; but these are the things you should have done without neglecting the others." Did that obligation cease a few days later when He died? Is the Christian not "under law to Christ," with His higher law of love? "I am not free from God's law," said Paul, "but am under Christ's law" (1 Cor. 9:21, NIV).

It would seem from an impartial weighing of the relevant Scriptures, that though there is no legal obligation resting on a believer to give a tithe, or more, of his income, his experience of Christ's matchless grace should provide a powerful incentive to emulate the example of his Master. As has been said, sacrifice is the ecstasy of giving the best we have to the One whom we love the most.

WHAT DID JESUS TEACH?

Because money is so often devoted to sordid ends, talking about it can be secular and sordid. But as with many other things, Jesus lifted it to a higher plane and showed how it could be transmuted into heavenly values.

He accorded to money an astounding prominence in His teaching. An analysis reveals that it figured in sixteen of His thirty-eight parables. One verse in six in the synoptic gospels has the same theme. Why did He give it such prominence?

■ Because money is one of the central realities of life,

and affects us all from cradle to grave. Jesus would have been unrealistic had He not given it due prominence.

- Because money is an acid test of character. Whether a person is rich or poor, discover his attitude to money, and you gain a deep insight into his character. One cannot be neutral where money is concerned.

- Because of its potential for good or evil. This obvious fact needs no elaboration.

Dr. Arthur T. Pierson has helpfully pointed out that our Lord enunciated several laws or principles in the realm of giving to God that deserve close attention.[3]

THE LAW OF STEWARDSHIP

Man is not an owner but a trustee of his money. That is made clear in several of Jesus' parables, for example Luke 12:42, the wise steward, and Luke 16:1-8, the unjust steward. It is not *one tenth* of our money that belongs to God, but *ten tenths*. The point at issue is not how much of *my money* I should give to God, but how much of *God's money* I should retain for the use of myself and my family. That may seem a radical concept, but then our Lord's teaching on the whole subject was radical too.

The wicked and slothful servant of Matthew 25:18 was judged for the way in which he exercised his stewardship of "his master's money." Do we regard our money as "our Master's money," or as our own? "He is Lord of all" (Acts 10:36), and it is our responsibility to administer faithfully what He has entrusted to us. The qualifications of a steward are that he be both "faithful and wise." That is, he will employ God's gifts to him with fidelity and sagacity, so as to provide increase for God.

THE LAW OF RECOMPENSE

"Give, and it will be given to you" (Luke 6:38). Both liberality and stinginess automatically bring their own reward. God has written it into universal law. The implication is that if we withhold His portion from God, He will withhold from us the spiritual blessing attached to it. If we are faithful stewards of the smaller gifts entrusted to us, that will open the way for Him to entrust us with more.

THE LAW OF PROPORTION

"Many rich people were putting in large sums. And a poor widow came and put in two small copper coins, which amount to a cent" (Mark 12:41-42). Jesus said to His disciples, "Truly I say to you, this poor widow put in more than all the contributors to the treasury" (v. 43). That is indeed the new mathematics, the arithmetic of heaven. God estimates our gifts not so much by their financial value, as by the sacrifice involved, the love that accompanies it, and the amount that is left. The supreme value of the widow's gift lay in the fact that she "out of her poverty, put in all she owned, all she had to live on"—while the others gave "out of their surplus" (Mark 12:44). Here is a searching test of our giving, but that incident should greatly encourage those who have only a little to give, but give it gladly.

THE LAW OF UNSELFISHNESS

"Lend, expecting nothing in return; and your reward will be great" (Luke 6:35). The underlying motive is the important thing here. *Why* I give is more important than *what* I give. It is sometimes said that it pays to be generous, and that is blessedly true. It is always better to be generous than to be mean. But, as that great philanthropist R. G. Le Tourneau said, "If you give because it pays, then it won't pay! That is trading, not giving, and God does not do business on that basis. No spiritual dividend accrues from such giving."

THE LAW OF TRANSMUTATION

"I say to you, make friends for yourselves, by means of the mammon of unrighteousness; that when it fails, they may receive you into the eternal dwellings" (Luke 16:9). Money, like the golden calf, very easily becomes an object of worship because of what it will procure for us. But the same golden calf can be melted down and transmuted into Bibles and books, into money that finances the Kingdom of God. The material can become spiritual and eternal. What surprises are ahead of us when the final day of transmutation comes! All earthly treasure can be changed into heavenly treasure. Let us give generously so that we will not go to a lonely heaven.

THE LAW OF SUPERIOR BLESSEDNESS

"It is more blessed to give than to receive" (Acts 20:35). By divine decree, what I give comes back to me in greater spiritual blessing.

An English nobleman who lay dying said remorsefully and self-censuringly,

> "What I spent, I had;
> What I kept, I lost;
> What I *gave* I have."

In those six laws or principles, we have a summary of Jesus' teaching on the subject.

What Did the Early Church Practice?

One might have expected the wealthy, richly gifted Corinthian church to be Paul's model. Instead, it was the poverty-stricken colonial church in Macedonia that demonstrated and experienced the superior blessedness of generous giving (2 Cor. 8:1-5).

They were remarkable people. In striking contrast to their deep poverty and affliction shone the riches of their abounding liberality. "That in a great ordeal of affliction their abundance of joy and their deep poverty overflowed in the wealth of their liberality" (v. 2). Despite their limited resources—for they were poor pioneers—they did not shrink from giving to the point of real sacrifice. They calculated the maximum they could give, and then went beyond it (v. 3). The question with them was not, "How little?" but, "How much?"

It is a common tendency even among Christians in our day to spend beyond the limit of our means, but have we ever emulated the Macedonians? "For I testify that according to their ability, and beyond their ability they gave of their own accord, begging us with much entreaty for the favor of participation in the support of the saints" (vv. 3-4).

What an extraordinary picture! The donor is the one who does the begging! The donor is the one who takes the initiative. Since they gave beyond the limit of their means, they were obviously looking to God to supply their other needs. They gave by principle, not by impulse. Their giving grew out of their surrender to Christ (v. 5).

The Macedonian Christians set us a noble example of liberality, with the result that they themselves were "exuberantly happy."

SATAN'S STRATEGY

Since money is one of the essentials of the work of the Kingdom, it is not surprising that the great adversary does all in his power to prevent it from finding its way into God's treasury, and for that he has many tricks in his bag.

He encourages overcommitment in buying: purchasing more than one can afford on time payments, so that there is little left over to give to God.

He plays on our competitive instincts and incites us to constantly upgrade our standard of living, so that increases in income are already committed. When John Wesley was earning £30 a year, he lived on £26 and gave the rest to God. When his salary was raised to £60, he lived on £26 and gave the rest to God.

He dries up the fountains of generosity in the heart by suggesting postponement of giving to some future time. The stifling of a generous impulse today makes it easier for us to do the same tomorrow.

He so arranges things that the assets of the generous man become frozen or over-committed, that he cannot give what he genuinely wishes to give. Expanding business too rapidly often demands reinvestment on a scale that leaves little for giving.

He encourages people to short-circuit present liberality through what Dr. A. J. Gordon styled *extra corpus benevolence*—the postponement of generosity until after death.

> Why is it that so many Christians make death their executor, leaving thousands and millions to be dispensed by his bony fingers? . . . It is doubtless wise to make modest provision for our dependents as we are able, but surely it cannot be termed Christian generosity when a man waits until death shakes it out of his pockets. Let us give all we can in our lifetime, and have the joy of seeing our money work for God. God promises a reward for "deeds done *in* the body," not out of it. To be generous with God from right motives brings its reward here as well as hereafter.

Let us aim to qualify for the blessedness promised in our Lord's ninth beatitude.

Notes

1. Charles C. Ryrie, *Balancing the Christian Life* (Chicago: Moody, 1969), p. 85.
2. Samuel Chadwick, "Concerning Christian Giving," *The Christian*, 3 February 1967, p. 14.
3. Arthur T. Pierson, "What Jesus Taught About Money," *Revelation*, August 1937, p. 329.

The supreme favor is that of being associated with Christ glorified in a fellowship so intimate, so tender, so glorious, and so useful, as is pictured by a bride and her husband.

This union will crown and complete the program of God for the universe. It will perfect the joy of the Son, for no union more intimate and sweet is known in creation. . . . And it is the highest honor that ever can be available for the redeemed, since the Bride sits with the Bridegroom on His throne, and God can never set anyone above His Son.[1]

G. H. Lang

17

Intimacy Is Consummated at the Advent

Revelation 19:1-10

The intimacy and closeness experienced during the engagement period is only the prelude to the much more joyous intimacy of married life. In many places, Scripture envisions the consummation of such a union between Christ and His chosen Bride. It is the event for which not only the believer but all heaven is waiting. It is the climax that the redeemed of every age have looked and longed for. It has formed the subject of glowing predictions of the prophets and the songs of the church, "the era for which creation groans, and the sons of God pray."

Before we consider "the wedding supper of the Lamb," it would be helpful to view the second coming of our Lord in the light of what it will mean to Him, for our intimacy with Him is not a one-sided thing.

The inherent selfishness of even the regenerate heart is seen in our tendency to view that event more in terms of how it will affect us, than of what it will mean to Him. We thrill at the thought of our inheritance in Christ, but are we equally thrilled at the thought of what "the riches of the glory of His inheritance in the saints" means to Him? (Eph. 1:18) Do we give sufficient thought to His eager expectation of His coronation day, His wedding day?

> He is waiting with long patience
>   For His crowning day,
> For that kingdom which shall never
>   Pass away.
> Watching till His royal banner
>   Floateth far and wide.
> Till He seeth of His travail,
>   Satisfied.
>
> A. J. Janvrin

A consideration of the startling contrasts between His first and second advents will heighten our appreciation of what the latter will mean to Him. Then He came in poverty and humiliation, now in inconceivable riches and glory. Then He came in weakness. Now He comes in power. Then He came in loneliness. Now He is accompanied by innumerable angels and the company of the redeemed. Then He came as a Man of sorrows, but now with radiant joy. Then in mockery the soldiers placed a reed in His hand as scepter. Now He receives and wields the scepter of universal dominion. Then men placed on His brow a crown of acanthus thorn. Now His brow is adorned with the many diadems He has won. Then He was blasphemed, denied, betrayed. Now every knee bows to Him, acknowledging Him as King of kings and Lord of lords.

Small wonder that Frances Ridley Havergal burst into doxology:

> O, the joy to see Thee reigning,
>   Thee, my own beloved Lord!
> Ev'ry tongue Thy name confessing,
>   Worship, honor, glory, blessing,
> Brought to Thee with one accord;
>   Thee, my Master and my Friend,
> Vindicated and enthron'd
>   Unto earth's remotest end
> Glorified, adored and owned.

When Jesus offered His sacerdotal prayer just before His death, He made only one personal request of His Father: "Father, I desire that they also, whom Thou has given Me, be with Me where I am, in order that they may behold My glory, which Thou hast given Me; for Thou didst love Me before the foundation of the world" (John 17:24). How amazing that the yearning of His heart was the continuation in heaven of the intimacy He had enjoyed with His people on earth!

When He comes again, that earnest desire will have its fulfilment. "Thus we shall always be with the Lord" (1 Thess. 4:17). He will be fully satisfied with the outcome of His costly sacrifice, for "He shall see of the travail of His soul and be satisfied" (Isa. 53:11, KJV).

The noted "Rabbi" Duncan of Edinburgh once preached on the text, "He shall see His seed" (Isa. 53:10, KJV). He divided his text as follows: (1) He shall see them born and brought in, (2) He shall see them educated and brought up, (3) He shall see them supported and brought through, (4) He shall see them glorified and brought home. This was part of "the joy set before Him."

When He returns, it will be to receive the Kingdom of which He had so much to say when on earth. When He came to His own people and offered Himself as their King, their response was in effect, "We will not have this man to reign over us." But at last His kingship will be universally acknowledged and confessed.

His glorious advent will issue in His eternal union with His Bride, the church which He purchased with His own blood. For Him, as for us, it will mean the ecstatic joy of "the wedding feast of the Lamb," and eternal mutual fellowship and communion.

The scene introducing the wedding opens with a grand hallelujah chorus being sung by a great heavenly choir. Their song attributes salvation, glory, and power to God because of His righteous judgment upon the wicked, persecuting harlot church (Rev. 19:2-4). It is a song of rejoicing in the triumph of truth over error. "And I heard, as it were, the voice of a great multitude and as the sound of many waters and as the sound of mighty peals of thunder, saying, 'Hallelujah! For the Lord our God, the Almighty, reigns' " (Rev. 19:6).

To their joy that the Lord God Almighty has now revealed Himself in full majesty and power, the members of the chorus exhort each other to greater rejoicing:

> "Let us rejoice and be glad and give the glory to Him. For the marriage of the Lamb has come and His Bride has made herself ready." And it was given her to clothe herself in fine linen, bright and clean; for the fine linen is the righteous acts of the saints. And he said to me, "Write, 'Blessed are those who are invited to the marriage supper of the Lamb.' " And he said to me, "These are the true words of God" (Rev. 19:7-9).

To understand the symbolism of that sublime scene, a background of knowledge of Eastern marriage customs is necessary. A Jewish betrothal was considered much more binding than is an engagement in our culture. In Jewish eyes, the betrothal couple were to all intents and purposes looked upon as married. Infidelity during the period of betrothal resulted in divorce.

During the period between betrothal and the wedding ceremony, the bridegroom paid the customary dowry to the father of the bride (e.g., Gen. 34:12). Then came the preparation and adornment of the bride who "made herself ready" for the great event. In company with his friends, the bridegroom proceeded to her home, received her, and accompanied her to his own home or that of his parents. The climax was the solemn, yet joyous, wedding feast.

The heavenly Bridegroom is, of course, the Lord Himself. The Bride of whom John the Baptist spoke is the true church, which includes all who have exercised saving faith. The marriage symbolism expresses the indissoluble union of Christ and His redeemed people.

Betrothal always has in view the wedding day, which is the happy climax to the growing communion and intimacy of courting days. The Bride of Christ was chosen in eternity. His incarnation made possible her betrothal to Him. He paid the bride-price, the dowry, in crimson drops of precious blood. Then followed the waiting time until He comes to take her to the glorious home He has prepared for her. During that time, the Bride is to make herself ready. The Bridegroom provides the wedding attire, the Bride arrays herself in it (Rev. 19:7-8).

Our Lord's two parables of the wedding feast underscore two important truths in connection with the need of preparation for the coming of the Bridegroom. In the parable of the wedding garment (Matt. 22:1-14), it is the need of personal holiness that is stressed. In the parable of the ten bridesmaids (Matt. 25:1-13), it is the need of being filled with the Holy Spirit. We must be sure that we have received the wedding garment, and that our lamps are filled with oil.

An Eastern wedding feast might last for a week, or even more. The wedding feast of the Lamb lasts throughout eternity. "And thus we shall always be with the Lord" (1 Thess. 4:17). A true marriage union is forever.

The eternal union of Christ and His church will be consummated in the home He has gone ahead to prepare for her. In preparing that eternal home for His loved ones, our Lord removes all that would spoil their enjoyment or cast gloom on their spirits. What will be absent from heaven? Tears, death, mourning, pain (Rev. 21:4), sickness (22:2), hunger (7:16), night (22:5), curse (22:3).

On the positive side there will be glory (21:23), light (22:5), unity (John 17:20-22), perfection (1 Cor. 13:9-10), joy (Psalm 16:11), love (1 Cor. 13:13), satisfaction (Psalm 17:15).

How will we be employed in heaven? Among others, these four activities will engage us:

WORSHIP AND ADORATION

We shall pay to the Triune God the worship that is His due. "The twenty-four elders"—representative of all redeemed humanity—"fall down before Him who sits on the throne, and will worship Him who lives forever and ever" (Rev. 4:10).

MUSIC

Music holds a prominent place in the imagery of heaven, as it did in the worship of Tabernacle and Temple. We are told that 288 musicians were employed in the Temple services (1 Chron. 25:1-8). Both vocal and instrumental music are cited as adding to the felicity of heaven. "The four living creatures and the twenty-four elders fell down before the Lamb, having each one of a harp. . . . And they sang a new song" (Rev. 5:8-9). If earthly choirs and orchestras can lift us to such heights of aesthetic enjoyment, what will the music of heaven be like?

SERVICE

"For this reason, they are before the throne of God; and they serve Him day and night in His temple" (7:15). Then we will have bodies like that of our Bridegroom and will know none of the limitations of time and space that now plague us. What endless vistas of possibility open before us as we think of ceaseless service for the One whom we love most.

FELLOWSHIP

"And they shall see His face, and His name shall be on their foreheads" (22:4). Few things on earth are more beautiful than the fellowship enjoyed by kindred spirits. In heaven, with all possible causes of discord and dissension excluded, we shall enjoy an infinite extension of the intimacy we have enjoyed with God on earth.[2]

Notes

1. G. H. Lang, *The Revelation of Jesus Christ* (London: Oliphants, 1945), p. 315.
2. J. Oswald Sanders, *The Certainty of Christ's Second Coming* (Manila: OMF Publishers, 1977).

Moody Press, a ministry of Moody Bible Institute, is designed for education, evangelization, and edification. If we may assist you in knowing more about Christ and the Christian life, please write us without obligation: Moody Press, c/o MLM, Chicago, Illinois 60610.

Steps to Peace with God

Step 1 | God's Purpose: Peace and Life

God loves you and wants you to experience peace and life—abundant and eternal.

The Bible Says . . .

". . . we have peace with God through our Lord Jesus Christ." Romans 5:1

"For God so loved the world that He gave His only begotten Son, that whoever believes in Him should not perish but have everlasting life." John 3:16

". . . I have come that they may have life, and that they may have it more abundantly." John 10:10b

Since God planned for us to have peace and the abundant life right now, why are most people not having this experience?

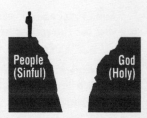

Step 2 | Our Problem: Separation

God created us in His own image to have an abundant life. He did not make us as robots to automatically love and obey Him, but gave us a will and a freedom of choice.

We chose to disobey God and go our own willful way. We still make this choice today. This results in separation from God.

Our choice results in separation from God.

The Bible Says . . .

"For all have sinned and fall short of the glory of God." Romans 3:23

"For the wages of sin is death, but the gift of God is eternal life in Christ Jesus our Lord." Romans 6:23

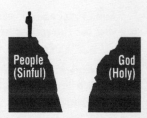

Our Attempts

Through the ages, individuals have tried in many ways to bridge this gap . . . without success . . .

The Bible Says . . .

"There is a way that seems right to man, but in the end it leads to death." Proverbs 14:12

"But your iniquities have separated you from God; and your sins have hidden His face from you, so that He will not hear." Isaiah 59:2

There is only one remedy for this problem of separation.

Step 3 God's Remedy: The Cross

Jesus Christ is the only answer to this problem. He died on the Cross and rose from the grave, paying the penalty for our sin and bridging the gap between God and people.

The Bible Says . . .

". . . God is on one side and all the people on the other side, and Christ Jesus, Himself man, is between them to bring them together . . ." 1 Timothy 2:5

"For Christ also has suffered once for sins, the just for the unjust, that He might bring us to God . . ." 1 Peter 3:18a

"But God demonstrates His own love for us in this: While we were still sinners, Christ died for us." Romans 5:8

God has provided the only way . . . we must make the choice . . .

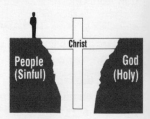

Step 4 Our Response: Receive Christ

We must trust Jesus Christ and receive Him by personal invitation.

The Bible Says . . .

"Behold, I stand at the door and knock. If anyone hears My voice and opens the door, I will come in to him and dine with him, and he with Me." Revelation 3:20

"But as many as received Him, to them He gave the right to become children of God, even to those who believe in His name." John 1:12

". . . if you confess with your mouth the Lord Jesus and believe in your heart that God has raised Him from the dead, you will be saved." Romans 10:9

Are you here . . . or here?

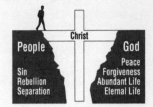

Is there any good reason why you cannot receive Jesus Christ right now?

How to receive Christ:

1. Admit your need (I am a sinner).
2. Be willing to turn from your sins (repent).
3. Believe that Jesus Christ died for you on the Cross and rose from the grave.
4. Through prayer, invite Jesus Christ to come in and control your life through the Holy Spirit. (Receive Him as Lord and Savior.)

What to Pray:

Dear Lord Jesus,

I know that I am a sinner and need Your forgiveness. I believe that You died for my sins. I want to turn from my sins. I now invite You to come into my heart and life. I want to trust and follow You as Lord and Savior.

In Jesus' name. Amen.

_____   _____
Date   Signature

God's Assurance:
His Word

If you prayed this prayer,

The Bible Says...

"For 'whoever calls upon the name of the Lord will be saved.'"
Romans 10:13

Did you sincerely ask Jesus Christ to come into your life? Where is He right now? What has He given you?

"**For it is by grace you have been saved, through faith—and this is not from yourselves, it is the gift of God—not by works, so that no one can boast.**" Ephesians 2:8,9

The
Bible Says...

"**He who has the Son has life; he who does not have the Son of God does not have life. These things I have written to you who believe in the name of the Son of God, that you may know that you have eternal life, and that you may continue to believe in the name of the Son of God.**" 1 John 5:12–13, NKJV

Receiving Christ, we are born into God's family through the supernatural work of the Holy Spirit who indwells every believer...this is called regeneration or the "new birth."

This is just the beginning of a wonderful new life in Christ. To deepen this relationship you should:

1. Read your Bible every day to know Christ better.
2. Talk to God in prayer every day.
3. Tell others about Christ.
4. Worship, fellowship, and serve with other Christians in a church where Christ is preached.
5. As Christ's representative in a needy world, demonstrate your new life by your love and concern for others.

God bless you as you do.

Billy Graham

If you want further help in the decision you have made, write to:
Billy Graham Evangelistic Association P.O. Box 779, Minneapolis, Minnesota 55440-0779